it's
not
teen edition
about
me
live like you mean it

max lucado

Published by
THOMAS NELSON
Since 1798

www.thomasnelson.com

Cover Design by DeAnna Pierce, Terra Petersen, Bill Chiaravalle—Brand Navigation, LLC
        www.brandnavigation.com
Cover Images by Frederic Tousche/Photographer's Choice, Michael Helssner/Stone

Interior Design by Joel Bartlett

Produced with the assistance of The Livingstone Corporation (www.Livingstonecorp.com). Project staff include Dave Veerman, Kirk Luttrell, and Joel Bartlett.

Library of Congress Cataloguing-in-Publication Data

Lucado, Max.
        It's not about me: live like you mean it / Max Lucado.— Teen ed.
            p. cm.
        Summary: "Max Lucado helps to free teens from the me-centric world they are used to living in and to help them set their sights on different goals by putting God at the center of their lives"—Provided by publisher.
        Includes bibliographical references.
        ISBN 13: 978-1-5914-5290-4
        ISBN 10: 1-5914-5290-2
1. Christian teenagers—Religious life. I Title: It's not about me.
II. Title.
        BV4531.3.L82 2005
        248.8'3—dc22
                                                                                            2005000082
Printed in the United States of America

07 08 09 RRD 5 4 3 2

To Kenny and Sharon Wilson

There may be a finer couple on this earth, but I haven't met them.
For your friendship, faith, and far too few hamburgers,
Denalyn and I say thank you.
We gladly dedicate this book to you:
two people who, because you already live it,
don't need to read it.

◖◭◮◗ *Contents* ◖◭◮◗

◎◎◎◎ *Acknowledgments* ◎◎◎◎

On a summer day in the late nineties I ran into a friend in a hotel lobby. Our last visit had occurred a year earlier. He had a few minutes. I had an empty stomach. So we bought deli sandwiches, found a table, and took a seat. "What has God been teaching you this year?" My question was expectation-free. But his answer gave me more than a sandwich to chew on.

"What has he been teaching me this year?" he reflected. "He's been teaching me that it's not about me."

The phrase stirred enough reflections to become a series of messages and, eventually, this book. So it's only right for me to pause and salute Sealy Yates. Thanks for sharing the line. More important, thanks for modeling it.

Sealy is not the only one who made this work possible. Here are some others:

Liz Heaney and Karen Hill—You so skillfully and gently recraft, clarify. Thanks to you, this book, and the one who wrote it, are in better shape.

Steve and Cheryl Green—Thanks for superintending my life and being our friends. Your comradeship means more to me than I can say.

Byron Williamson, Joey Paul, Laura Minchew and the young people who shared their stories for this special teen edition—I'm grateful.

Dylan Connell—Thanks for contributing your "teen" perspective on this edition.

My Peak of the Week family—You let me guinea pig this material on you. How kind you were to stay awake.

Carol Bartley—No one does it better. Your penchant for grammatical precision astounds us all.

Dwight Edwards—*Revolution Within* connected the dots for me.

John Piper—Reading *The Supremacy of God in Preaching* was like seeing a map of the solar system for the first time. Thanks for reminding me of my place.

Dean Merrill—Thanks for graciously squaring the facts.

Rick Atchley—Thanks for the great messages, for being a great friend.

Charles Prince—Thanks for untangling theological knots and sharing a lifetime of knowledge.

Jenna, Andrea, and Sara—my daughters, my treasures.

Denalyn, my wife—Vienna had Mozart. I have you. What music you bring into my life.

And most of all to you, Author of life. What a great God you are. It's all about you. Period.

But all of us who are Christians . . .
reflect like mirrors the glory of the Lord.

2 Corinthians 3:18 PHILLIPS

Foreword

NBA championship teams have something in common: they play with one goal in mind. Each player contributes his own gifts and efforts so that the greater goal—winning—can be reached. But players who seek their own glory at the sacrifice of the team's glory drive the team away from success. So it is with life. The goal is not our own glory. In fact, trying to make life "all about us" pushes happiness further out of reach.

Our society is not wired for this kind of thinking. It's a me-centric world out there, which destroys much of what should be good. Marriages are ruined because one or both partners are focused on their own happiness. Successful men and women are ruined by their own success, believing they don't need anyone else's input. And for some, life's troubles are magnified because they believe life is all about them.

The Bible is full of men and women who struggled with me-centric thinking, so our generation is not alone. If we would learn from them, we could live in freedom. We would be able to enjoy our successes without taking the credit, like King David. We could bear up under troubles with confidence in God, like Job. By letting go of our own agendas and timetables, as Moses finally did, we would discover that God's plans are mind-blowing. In the end, a God-centric lifestyle would free us to live life to the fullest!

My friend Max Lucado has years of experience in following God, which is why I am happy to recommend this book. If you want a great meal, I'll send you to a great chef. But if you want to learn about God's ways, I'll send you to someone who has walked with Him for a long while.

Max is such a man; the Lord has prepared him for just this purpose. I encourage you to read with an open heart as Max shares the joy of a God-centered life.

May God free us all from me-centric living. All the glory is His!

David Robinson
Former NBA Player

chapter 1

bumping life off self-center

Blame the bump on Copernicus.

Until Copernicus came along in 1543, we earthlings enjoyed center stage. Fathers could place an arm around their children, point to the night sky, and proclaim, "The universe revolves around us."

Ah, the hub of the planetary wheel, the navel of the heavenly body, the White House of the cosmos. Ptolemy's second-century finding had convinced us. Stick a pin in the center of a map of the stars, and you've found the earth. Dead center.

And, what's more, dead still! Let the other planets wander through the skies. Not us. No sir. We stay put. As predictable as Christmas. No orbiting. No rotating. Some fickle planets revolve 180 degrees from one day to the next. Not ours. As budgeless as the Rock of Gibraltar. Let's hear loud applause for the earth, the anchor of the universe.

But then came Nicolaus. Nicolaus Copernicus with his maps, drawings, bony nose, Polish accent, and pestering questions. Oh, those questions he asked.

"Ahem, can anyone tell me what causes the seasons to change?"

"Why do some stars appear in the day and others at night?"

"Does anyone know exactly how far ships can sail before falling off the edge of the earth?"

"Trivial stuff!" people scoffed. "Who has time for such problems?"

But Copernicus persisted. Pointing a lone finger toward the sun, he announced, "Behold the center of the solar system."

People denied the facts for over half a century. When like-minded Galileo came along, the throne locked him up, and the church kicked him out. You'd have thought he had called the king a stepchild or the pope a Baptist.

People didn't take well to demotions back then.

We still don't.

What Copernicus did for the earth, God does for our souls. He points to the Son—his Son—and says, "Behold the center of it all."

③

> God raised him [Christ] from death and set him on a throne in deep heaven, in charge of running the universe, everything from galaxies to governments, no name and no power exempt from his rule. And not just for the time being but *forever*. He is in charge of it all, has the final word on everything. At the center of all this, Christ rules the church. (Ephesians 1:20–22 MSG)

When God looks at the center of the universe, he doesn't look at you. When heaven's stagehands direct the spotlight toward the star of the show, I need no sunglasses. No light falls on me.

> When **God** looks at the center of the **universe**, he doesn't look at you.

Lesser orbs, that's us. Appreciated. Valued. Loved dearly.

But central? Essential? Critical? Nope. Sorry. The world does not revolve around us. Our comfort is not God's priority.

If it is, something's gone wrong. If we are the primary event, how do we explain challenges like death, disease, or rumbling earthquakes? If God exists to please us, then shouldn't we always be pleased?

Could a Copernicus-type shift be in order? Perhaps our place is not at the center of the universe. God does not exist to make a big deal out of us. We exist to make a big deal out of him. It's not about you. It's not about me. It's all about him.

The moon models our role.

> If **God** exists to please us, then shouldn't we **always** be pleased?

What does the moon do? She generates no light. Contrary to the lyrics of the song, this harvest moon cannot shine on. Apart from the sun, the moon is nothing more than a pitch-black, pockmarked rock. But properly positioned, the moon beams. Let her do what she was made to do, and a clod of dirt becomes a source of inspiration and romance. The moon reflects the greater light.

 And she's happy to do so! You never hear the moon complaining. She makes no waves about making waves. Let the cow jump over her or astronauts step on her; she never objects. Even though sunning is accepted while mooning is the butt of bad jokes, you won't hear ol' Cheeseface grumble. The moon is at peace in her place. And because she is, soft light touches a dark earth.

What would happen if we accepted our place as Son reflectors?

Perhaps something like this:

Erin Curry
Baptist Press News
August 26, 2004

At just eighteen, Allyson Felix has broken world records in the 200-meter race and narrowly missed a gold medal at the Olympics.

What's more, Allyson sees her running ability as a gift from God.

Allyson, daughter of an ordained minister and professor of New Testament at the Master's Seminary in Sun Valley, California, captured the Olympic silver medal in the women's 200 meters on August 25, 2004, by setting a world junior record of 22.18 seconds. She was just behind Veronica Campbell of Jamaica, who won the gold medal in 22.05 seconds, and just ahead of Debbie Ferguson of the Bahamas, who took the bronze in 22.30 seconds.

But when Allyson won the silver, she didn't seem to grasp the significance. "I don't think she realized what she accomplished," her father, Paul, said after watching his daughter simply walk off the track after the race. "If she had, she would have taken a victory lap."

Allyson, who broke Marion Jones's record for the fastest time in a high school competition in 2003, told the Associated Press she was happy with her finish. "I have a lot of confidence, and

I'm very excited about the future," she said. But even more important is what she said in an interview with *Today's Christian Woman* magazine. Allyson said that God "gave me this ability. My speed is definitely a gift from Him, and I run for His glory. Whatever I do, He allows me to do it."

Allyson's success hasn't come without setbacks. During her junior year of high school, Felix pulled a hamstring at the state championships and reinjured it a few weeks later at the U.S. Junior National Championships. By the time she made it to the World Juniors in Jamaica, she had lost her edge and ended up in fifth place. News articles said Allyson had choked, but she kept her head up. "That was an extremely hard time," she said. "I had to depend on God."

Paul Felix said his daughter's faith is an important part of balancing the pressures that come with being a world-class runner. "We try to help Allyson keep things in perspective by looking at life from God's point of view. The reality is Allyson can get from point A to point B faster than most people, and our society has put a big emphasis on that. But that is not significant in light of eternity. So we try to remind her that God has given her this ability, and she is responsible for using it to His glory."

During the time she was hurt and could not fully run, Allyson had to depend on God—a practice she continues as an elementary education major at the University of Southern California by trying "to make time every day to spend in the Word and in prayer." She says, "I'm going to FCA [Fellowship of Christian Athletes] meetings, and I'm attending church regularly. My faith means everything to me, and in every way, my goal is to bring God the glory."[1]

Allyson is a Son reflector. Her goal is not to absorb the glory but to reflect it back to her Maker.

For most of us, such a shift doesn't come easily, however. We've been demanding our way and stamping our feet since infancy. Aren't we all born with a default drive set on selfishness? *I want a family that lets me have my way and friends who always agree with me. It's all about me.*

> **Aren't** we urged to look out for **number one?**

Promote me. Take care of me. Focus on me. It's all about me!

Aren't we urged to look out for number one? Find our place in the sun? Make a name for ourselves? We thought celebrating ourselves would make us happy . . .

But what chaos this philosophy creates. If you think it's all about you, and I think it's all about me, we have no hope for getting along.

What would happen if we took our places and played our parts in this universe? If we played the parts God gave us to play? If that was our highest priority?

Would we see a change in our families? We'd certainly *hear* a change. Less "Here is what I want!" More "What do you suppose God wants?"

What if you took that approach? Goals of being popular and part of the in-crowd—you'd shelve them. God-reflecting would dominate.

And your body? Ptolemy-type thinking says, "It's mine; I'm going to enjoy it." God-centered thinking acknowledges, "It's God's; I have to respect it."

You'd see suffering differently. "My pain proves God's absence" would be replaced with "My pain expands God's purpose."

Talk about a Copernican shift. Talk about a healthy shift. Life makes sense when we accept our place. The gift of pleasures, the purpose of problems—all for him. The God-centered life works. And it rescues us from a life that doesn't.

But how do we make the shift? How can we be bumped off self-center? Attend a class, howl at the moon, read a Lucado book? None of these (though the author appreciates that last idea). We move from me-focus to God-focus by pondering him. Witnessing him. Following the counsel of the apostle Paul: "Beholding as in a glass the glory of the Lord, [we] are changed into the same image from glory to glory, even as by the Spirit of the Lord" (2 Corinthians 3:18 KJV).

Beholding him changes us. Couldn't we use a change? Let's give it a go. Who knows? We might just discover our place in the universe.

◎◎◎◎ *a thought question* ◎◎◎◎

*If strangers looked at your belongings,
your activities, and your actions, who would
they see at the center of your universe?*

Now live like you mean it.
Answer the questions on page 142.

part one

God-pondering

1

chapter 2

show me your glory

An anxious Moses needs help. This one-time shepherd has just conducted the largest mass exodus in history, leading a million people out of Egypt, out of slavery—and straight into a wilderness. To say the least, things haven't gone smoothly. So Moses pleads with God for help. "Look, you tell me, 'Lead this people,' but you don't let me know whom you're going to send with me. . . . Are you traveling with us or not?" (Exodus 33:12, 16 MSG).

His Maker offers assurance. "I myself will go with you. . . . I will do what you ask, because I know you very well, and I am pleased with you" (vv. 14, 17 NCV).

You'd think that would have been enough for Moses, but he lingers. Thinking, perhaps, of that last sentence: "I will do what you ask . . ." Perhaps God will allow one more request. So Moses swallows, sighs, and requests . . .

What do you think he will ask for? He has God's attention. God seems willing to hear his prayer.

So many requests he could make. There are a million stiff-necked, unappreciative, cow-worshiping ex-slaves in his rearview mirror who grumble with every step (Exodus 12:37). Had Moses prayed, "Could you turn these people into sheep?", who would have blamed him?

And what about Israel's enemies? Battlefields in Canaan lie ahead. Combat with Hittites, Jebusites . . . Termites, and Cellulites. They infest the land. Can Moses mold an army out of pyramid-building Hebrews? Had Moses prayed, "Could you just beam us to Canaan?", who would have blamed him?

Moses knew what God could do. The entire Ancient East knew. They were still talking about Aaron's staff becoming a snake and the Nile becoming blood. The plagues had brought air so thick with gnats you breathed them. Ground so layered with locusts you crunched them. Noonday blackness. Hail-pounded crops. Flesh covered with boils. Funerals for the firstborn.

God had even turned the Red Sea into a red carpet. Yes, Moses knew what God could do.

So with grumbling Israelites behind him and dangerous Canaanites in front of him, what is Moses' one request to God? "Show me your glory" (Exodus 33:18 NCV).

> We cross a line when we make such a request. When our deepest desire is not the things of God, or a favor from God, but God himself, we cross a threshold. Less self-focus, more God-focus. Less about me, more about him.

"Show me your radiance," Moses is praying. "Flex your biceps. Let me see the *S* on your chest. Your preeminence. Your heart-stopping, ground-shaking extraspectacularness. Forget good looks and athletic ability. Bypass the great GPA. I can live without them, but I can't live without you. I want more God, please. I'd like to see more of your glory."

Why did Moses want to see God's greatness?

Ask yourself a similar question. Why do you stare at sunsets and ponder the summer night sky? Why do you search for a rainbow in the mist or gaze at the Grand Canyon? How do we explain our fascination with such sights?

Beauty? Yes. But doesn't the beauty point to a beautiful Someone? Doesn't the immensity of the ocean suggest an immense Creator? Doesn't the rhythm of migrating cranes and beluga whales hint of a brilliant mind? And isn't that what we desire? A beautiful Maker? An immense Creator? A God so mighty that he can commission the birds and command the fish?

"Show me your glory, God." This is the prayer of Moses.

And God answers it. He places his servant in the cleft of a rock, telling Moses, "You cannot see My face; for no man shall see Me, and live. . . . I . . . will cover you with My hand while I pass by. Then I will take away My hand, and you shall see My back; but My face shall not be seen" (Exodus 33:20, 22–23 NKJV).

> "Show me your glory, **God**." This is the prayer of **Moses**.

And so Moses, cowering beneath the umbrella of God's palm, waits, surely with face bowed, eyes covered, and pulse racing, until God gives the signal. When the hand lifts, Moses' eyes do the same and catch a distant, disappearing glance of the back of God. The heart and center of the Maker is too much for Moses to bear. A fading glimpse will have to do. I'm seeing the long gray hair of Moses wind-whipped forward and his leathery hand grabbing a rock in the wall so he won't fall. And as the dust settles and his locks rest again on his shoulders, we see the impact. His face. Gleaming. Bright as if backlit by a thousand torches. Unknown to Moses, but undeniable to the Israelites, is his shimmering face. When he descended the mountain, "the sons of Israel could not look intently at the face of Moses because of the glory of his face" (2 Corinthians 3:7).

Witnesses saw not anger in his jaw, or worry in his eyes, or a scowl on his lips; they saw God's glory in his face.

Not Moses' glory. But God's glory in Moses' face.

Don't we, too, sometimes see God's glory in people's faces?

If you follow basketball, you've likely heard of David Robinson. This seven-foot-tall basketball player for the San Antonio Spurs was good. For fourteen seasons he dominated the league: MVP, All-Star, two championship rings, two Olympic gold medals. But it was his character that caught the attention of the public. These words appeared in the *Washington Times* the day after Robinson's departing championship victory.

> Robinson showed that a player did not have to be cheap or dirty to be effective. He did not have to clutter his body with tattoos or litter the NBA cities with illegitimate children. Robinson never felt a need to bring attention to himself, to shimmy after a good play or point to the crowd, as if to say, "Look at me. Aren't I something special?"
>
> The good guys won. Robinson won. Decency won. We all won.[1]

Minutes after hoisting the trophy overhead, David was interviewed by a national network. "People in San Antonio know what I'm going to say," he told the reporter. And we did. We did because we had heard him say it and seen him live it for so long. "All the glory goes to God," he announced.

Reflecting the glory of God. That was David Robinson's goal. And if we look at a group of teens from Iowa, we can catch a glimpse of God's glory reflected in them as well.

Krista Bjorn
Merced Sun Star
August 14, 2004

In the last weeks before school starts up again, manual labor in the hot sun is the last thing most high school students want to do. Yet recently, the youth group from Park Church of Christ in Goldfield, Iowa, traveled almost two thousand miles to serve the city of Merced, California, in whatever way they could.

"They just wanted to do something that might make a little bit of a difference," said Chris Medina, senior pastor at Christian Church of the Valley in Merced. "We also want to continue the ministry that [Jesus] pioneered during his life: serving others. That was just as much a part of his ministry as teaching about the Lord."

The group's first day of service was working alongside Habitat for Humanity volunteers, helping to do plastering, taping, and texturing. On their second day, the young people woke bright and early to clean up the skate park at Applegate Park. Grasping rollers and gallons of gray paint, the youth group turned the dirty, pockmarked, color-strewn surfaces into a clean and welcoming environment for Merced skateboarders. The kids also picked up garbage around the park and painted over graffiti left on trash cans and other surfaces.

The following weekend the young people were back with the Habitat for Humanity folks, donating their time, skills, and labor to build a home for a needy family.

"If it can help somebody else out, that's what I'm here for," said sixteen-year-old Heather Willis. "God wants us to help others."

"It's fun to offer help and see that it does affect others," said seventeen-year-old Nikita Clay, who became a Christian in 2002 and has found her life and focus completely altered as a result. "I do everything because of [God], because He's given me His grace. He's always been there for me, my best friend through it all. I know I can always turn to Him, and it's a very comforting thing."

"God wants us to do this," said sixteen-year-old Michael Shindelar. "It says in the Bible, 'Go minister My Word.' It's pretty much all about Him."[2]

Forgive my being so direct, but if it's all about God, shouldn't Moses' request be yours? Wouldn't you like a glimpse of God's glory?

Look at you. You've got problems. Living in a dying body, walking on a decaying planet, surrounded by a self-centered society. Pain. War. Disease.

These are no small issues. A small god? No thanks. You and I need what Moses needed—a glimpse of God's glory. Such a sighting can change you forever.

In the early pages of my childhood memory, I see this picture: My father and I sit side by side in a chapel. We both wear our only suits. The shirt collar rubs my neck; the pew feels hard to my bottom; the sight of my dead uncle leaves us all silent. This is my first funeral. My nine years of life have not prepared me for death. What I see unnerves me. Aunts, typically jovial and talkative, weep loudly. Uncles, commonly quick with a word and joke, stare wide-eyed at the casket. And Buck, my big uncle with meaty hands, big belly, and booming voice, lies whitish and waxy in the coffin.

I remember my palms moistening and my heart bouncing in my chest like tennis sneakers in a clothes dryer. Fear had me in her talons. What other emotion could I feel? Where do I look? The weeping ladies frighten me. Glassy-eyed men puzzle me. My dead uncle spooks me. But then I look up. I see my father.

He turns his face toward me and smiles softly. "It's okay, son," he assures, laying a large hand on my leg. Somehow I know it is. Why it is, I don't know. My family still wails. Uncle Buck is still dead. But if Dad, in the midst of it all, says it's okay, then that's enough.

At that moment I realized something. I could look around and find fear, or look at my father and find faith.

I chose my father's face.

So did Moses.

So can you.

◁△▽▷ *a thought question* ◁△▽▷

*What are you most afraid of,
and how could you turn that fear into faith?*

(21)

**Now *live* like you mean it.
Answer the questions on pages 143–144.**

chapter 3

divine self-promotion

Moses asked to see it on Sinai.

It billowed through the temple, leaving priests too stunned to minister.

When Ezekiel saw it, he had to bow.

It encircled the angels and starstruck the shepherds in the Bethlehem pasture.

Jesus radiates it.

John beheld it.

Peter witnessed it on Transfiguration Hill.

Christ will return enthroned in it.

Heaven will be illuminated by it.[1]

It floods Scripture, touching every person with the potential of changing every life. Including yours. One glimpse, one taste, one sampling, and your faith will never be the same . . .

Glory.

God's glory.

To seek God's glory is to pray, "Thicken the air with your presence; make it misty with your majesty. Part heaven's drapes, and let your nature spill forth. God, show us God."

> To ask to see God's **glory** is to ask to see **all** of God.

What the word *Alps* does for the mountains of Europe, *glory* does for God's nature. *Alps* encompasses a host of beauties: creeks, peaks, falling leaves, running elk. To ask to see the Alps is to ask to see it all. To ask to see God's glory is to ask to see all of God. God's glory carries the full weight of his attributes: his love, his character, his strength, and on and on.

David celebrated God's glory.

> Bravo, GOD, bravo!
>> Gods and all angels shout, "Encore!"
> In awe before the glory,
>> in awe before God's visible power.
> Stand at attention!
>> Dress your best to honor him!
>
> GOD thunders across the waters,
> Brilliant, his voice and his face, streaming
>> brightness—
> GOD, across the flood waters. . . .
>
> GOD's thunder spits fire.
> GOD thunders, the wilderness quakes;
> He makes the desert of Kadesh shake.
>
> GOD's thunder sets the oak trees dancing
> A wild dance, whirling; the pelting rain strips
>> their branches.
> We fall to our knees—we call out, "Glory!"
>> (Psalm 29:1–3, 7–9 MSG)

The word signals high honor. The Hebrew term for *glory* descends from a root word meaning "heavy, weighty, or important." God's glory, then, celebrates his significance, his uniqueness, his one-of-a-kindness. As Moses prayed, "Who among the gods is like you, O LORD? Who is like you—majestic in holiness, awesome in glory, working wonders?" (Exodus 15:11 NIV).

25

When you think "God's glory," think "priority." For God's glory is God's priority.

> God's team meetings, if he had them, would revolve around one question: "How can we reveal my glory today?" God's to-do list consists of one item: "Reveal my glory." Your homework from heaven? One item: "Declare God's glory."

God exists to showcase God.

He told Moses: "By those who come near Me I must be regarded as holy; and before all the people I must be glorified" (Leviticus 10:3 NKJV).

Why did he harden Pharaoh's heart? "I will harden Pharaoh's heart, and he will pursue them [the Israelites]. But I will gain glory for myself through Pharaoh and all his army, and the Egyptians will know that I am the LORD" (Exodus 14:4 NIV).

Why do the heavens exist? The heavens exist to "declare the glory of God" (Psalm 19:1 NIV).

Why did God choose the Israelites? Through Isaiah he called out to "everyone who is called by My name, whom I have created for My glory" (Isaiah 43:7 NKJV).

Why do people struggle? God answers, "I have tested you in the furnace of affliction. For My own sake, for My own sake, I will act" (Isaiah 48:10–11). "Trust me in your times of trouble, and I will rescue you, and you will give me glory" (Psalm 50:15 NLT).

Christ taught us to make God's reputation our priority in prayer: "Our Father who is in heaven, hallowed be Your name" (Matthew 6:9).

Every act of heaven reveals God's glory. Every act of Jesus did the same. Indeed, "The Son reflects the glory of God" (Hebrews 1:3 NCV). The night before his crucifixion, Jesus declared, "Now my heart is troubled, and what shall I say? 'Father, save me from this hour'? No, it was

> **Every** act of heaven reveals God's **glory**.

for this very reason I came to this hour. Father, glorify your name!" (John 12:27–28 NIV). Paul explains that "Christ has become a servant of the Jews . . . so that the Gentiles may glorify God for his mercy" (Romans 15:8–9 NIV).

And Jesus declared his mission a success by saying, "I have brought you glory on earth by completing the work you gave me to do" (John 17:4 NIV).

God has one goal: God. "I have my reputation to keep up" (Isaiah 48:11 MSG).

Surprised? Isn't such an attitude, dare we ask, self-centered? Don't we deem this behavior "self-promotion"? Why does God broadcast himself?

For the same reason the pilot of the lifeboat does. Think of it this way. You're floundering neck-deep in a dark, cold sea. Ship sinking. Life jacket deflating. Strength fading. Through the inky night comes the voice of a lifeboat pilot. But you cannot see him. What do you want the driver of the lifeboat to do?

Be quiet? Say nothing? Sneak his way through the drowning passengers? By no means! You need volume! Amp it up, buddy! In biblical jargon, you want him to show his glory. You need to hear him say, "I am here. I am strong. I have room for you. I can save you!" Drowning passengers want the pilot to announce his presence.

Don't we want God to do the same? Look around. People thrash about in seas of guilt, anger, despair. Life isn't working. We are going down fast. But God can rescue us. And only one message matters. His! We need to see God's glory.

Seventeen-year-old Austin says, "I was getting into deep water, and he reeled me back in."

Aimee Courtice,
Young Life's *Relationships* magazine
Spring 2003

Austin Meyer loves baseball. And even though Texas is his home, he isn't a fan of the Texas Rangers or the Houston Astros. His pick: the Chicago Cubs. "They're the lovable losers," he said. "I like to watch the underdogs win."

Maybe that's because Austin knows how to persevere when the odds are stacked against him.

Three years ago Austin was on his school's junior varsity baseball team and enjoying life as a high school student. Then, in February of 2001, Austin had a stroke while playing in a baseball game. "When I was in the hospital, my neuro-surgeon wasn't hopeful. He said, 'He'll probably never open his eyes.' But what I am about is proving people wrong."

Austin opened his eyes, but the stroke resulted in impaired movement of the left side of his body. Since then, he has worked diligently in physical and speech therapy. And although he hasn't recovered completely, Austin is an active high school student—hanging out with his friends, playing Ultimate Frisbee, going to the prom, and thinking about college.

Last spring, as Austin fought for physical recovery, a different kind of restoration was taking place—one even Austin had not hoped for.

Young Life club had started for Lake Travis High School in Austin, Texas, and Austin's friends were going. Club was fun for him, so he continued to go. Throughout that semester, Austin paid increasing attention to what the leaders talked about at the end of club.

Before then, Austin had never thought much about God. He was pretty sure God existed—but he didn't consider really needing God or a relationship with him. Then at one of the last clubs of the semester, a leader talked about Jesus's crucifixion. Hearing about Jesus's physical torment pierced Austin's heart. Austin was learning how to live with a changed body, but that night at Young Life he was faced with the scorned and tortured body of Jesus. "I knew he died on a cross, but hearing about the pain he went through, I thought, 'Why not believe in him?'"

Austin's journey with Jesus began that night, and when he went to camp at Frontier Ranch in Colorado that summer, he experienced Christ's power demonstrated in him. On the fourth day of camp, everyone was headed on a five-hour hike up nearby Chrysolite Mountain, not an easy feat for any teenager. Leaders and campers from Lake Travis High School offered to carry Austin the entire way. Austin refused. "I didn't think I could hike it," Austin said. "But I really wanted to."

Maggie Clark, who is on staff at Lake Travis, and Chris Trevathan, a leader, hiked the entire way with Austin. With Austin's arms wrapped around their shoulders, they pressed on, up steep switchbacks and over sometimes icy and slippery ground. For Austin, the key was to focus on each step, not the entire path ahead.

The trail narrowed, and the air became thinner. But Clark and the rest stuck close to Austin. At the top of the mountain a large group of campers clapped and cheered for him. "I felt like the hero of the camp," Austin said. "God was using me to show me how great he is."

A year earlier that kind of challenge had been impossible for Austin. Now he knew he had more than just his friends by his side—he had the help of the ultimate guide and companion. "There was someone with me the whole time," he said.

And not only did Austin hike up the mountain, but he also hiked down it. "He made it all the way down," Clark said. "This has given him such encouragement and life. He never thought he'd be able to do anything like that in his life, and God has redeemed that. He finds his confidence in the Lord now. He knows he can't make it through life without God."

Austin knows life for him will not always be a mountaintop experience. But he is confident of God's hand in his life. "I hope I will get back 100 percent of how I was, but with God I know he can do anything," Austin said. "He's everything to me. I know, with him, I don't have to worry. . . . My accident was a sign of him. I was getting into deep water, and he reeled me back in."

Charlie McCallie, Austin's Young Life leader, says that Austin continues to grow in his relationship with the Lord. He's also a regular at Campaigners and spends time with his lost friends. "He's really learned to put his life in God's hands. He has a hope outside of what the doctors tell him."[2]

Make no mistake: God has no ego problem. *He does not reveal his glory for his good. We need to witness it for ours.* Like Austin, we need a strong hand to pull us into a safe boat. And, once aboard, what becomes our priority?

Simple. Promote God. We declare that he is more important than anything else in life. "Hey! Strong boat over here! Able pilot! He can pull you out!"

Passengers promote the pilot. "Not to us, O LORD, not to us, but to Your name give glory because of Your lovingkindness, because of Your truth" (Psalm 115:1). If we boast at all, we "boast in the Lord" (2 Corinthians 10:17).

The breath you took as you read that last sentence was given to you for one reason: that you might for another moment "reflect the Lord's glory" (2 Corinthians 3:18 NIV). God awoke you and me this morning for one purpose: "Declare his glory among the nations, his marvelous deeds among all peoples" (1 Chronicles 16:24 NIV).

"God made all things, and everything continues through him and *for* him. To him be the glory forever" (Romans 11:36 NCV; emphasis mine). "There is only one God, the Father, who created everything, and *we exist for him*" (1 Corinthians 8:6 NLT; emphasis mine).

Why does the earth spin? For him.

Why do you have talents and abilities? For him.

Strength or struggles? For him.

Everything and everyone exists to reveal his glory.

Including you.

◀◉◉▶ *a thought question* ◀◉◉▶

Take a serious look at something you struggle with. Illness? Loneliness? Family pressures? How can you use that struggle for God's glory?

Now *live* like you mean it.
Answer the questions on pages 145–146.

chapter 4

holy
different

Frederick Dellenbaugh was only eighteen when he joined Major Powell on his pioneering river voyages through the Grand Canyon. Led by the one-armed Powell, the explorers floated on leaky boats and faced high waters. It's a wonder they survived. It's every bit as much a wonder what they saw. Frederick described the scene:

> My back being towards the fall I could not see it. . . . Nearer and nearer came the angry tumult; the Major shouted "Back water!" there was a sudden dropping away of all support; then the mighty wavers [sic] smote us. The boat rose to them well, but we were flying at twenty-five miles an hour and at every leap the breakers rolled over us. "Bail!" shouted the Major,—"Bail for your lives!" and we dropped the oars to bail, though bailing was almost useless. . . . The boat rolled and pitched like a ship in a tornado. . . . canopies of foam pour[ed] over gigantic black boulders, first on one side, then on the other. . . . If you will take a watch and count by it ninety seconds, you will probably have about the time we were in this chaos, though it seemed much longer to me. Then we were through.[1]

Frederick knew rapids. Rivers and raging water were not new to him. But something about this river was. The sudden immensity, stark intensity—something stole the oarsman's breath. He knew rapids. But none like this. He was awestruck.

Skip way back in time to the prophet Isaiah. Facefirst on the temple floor. Arms crossed above his head. Muffled voice crying for mercy. Like Frederick, he's awe-struck. But unlike

Frederick, he's seen more than creation—he's seen the Creator. He's seen God.

Seven and one-half centuries before Christ, Isaiah was ancient Israel's version of a Senate chaplain or court priest. His family, aristocratic. His Hebrew, perfect. Polished, professional, and successful. But the day he saw God only one response seemed appropriate: "Woe is me, for I am ruined." What caused such a confession? What stirred such a reply? The answer is found in the word repeated three times by the seraphim: "Holy, Holy, Holy."

Seraphim stood above Him, each having six wings: with two he covered his face, and with two he covered his feet, and with two he flew. And one called out to another and said,

> "Holy, Holy, Holy, is the Lord of hosts,
> The whole earth is full of His glory."

> And the foundations of the thresholds trembled at the voice of him who called out, while the temple was filling with smoke. Then I said,

> "Woe is me, for I am ruined!
> Because I am a man of unclean lips,
> And I live among a people of
> unclean lips;

> For my eyes have seen the King, the
> Lord of hosts." (Isaiah 6:2–5)

The seraphim, those six-winged angels, proclaimed three times the same word. "Holy, holy, holy is the LORD Almighty" (NIV). Repetition, in Hebrew, performs the work of our highlighter. A tool of emphasis. God is not holy. He is not holy, holy. He is holy, holy, holy.

What other attribute receives such enforcement? No verse describes God as "wise, wise, wise" or "strong, strong, strong." Only as "holy, holy, holy." God's holiness commands headline attention. The adjective qualifies his name more than all others combined.[2] The first and final songs of the Bible magnify the holiness of God. Having crossed the Red Sea, Moses and the Israelites sang, "Who among the gods is like you, O LORD? Who is like you—majestic in holiness, awesome in glory, working wonders?" (Exodus 15:11 NIV). In Revelation those who have been victorious over the beast sing, "Who will not fear you, O Lord, and bring glory to your name? For you alone are holy" (15:4 NIV).

> **God** is not holy. He is not holy, holy. He is **holy, holy, holy**.

The Hebrew word for *holy* is *qadosh,* which means "cut off or separate." Holiness, then, speaks of the "otherness" of God. His total uniqueness. Everything about God is different from the world he has made.

What you are to a paper airplane, God is to you. Take a sheet of paper and make one. Contrast yourself with your creation. Challenge it to a spelling contest. Who will win? Dare it to race you around the block. Who is faster? Invite the airplane to a game of one-on-one basketball. Will you not dominate the court?

And well you should. The thing has no brainwaves, no pulse. It exists only because you formed it and flies only when someone throws it. Multiply the contrasts between you and the paper plane by infinity, and you will begin to catch a glimpse of the disparity between God and us.

> **Holiness**, then, speaks of the **"otherness"** of God

Even God asks, "To whom will you compare me? Who is my equal?" (Isaiah 40:25 NLT). As if his question needed an answer, he gives one:

> I am God—I alone! I am God, and there is no one else like me. Only I can tell you what is going to happen even before it happens. Everything I plan will come to pass, for I do whatever I wish. I will call a swift bird of prey from the east—a leader from a distant land who will come and do my bidding. I have said I would do it, and I will. (Isaiah 46:9–11 NLT)

Any search for a godlike person or position on earth is useless. No one and nothing compare with him. No one advises him. No one helps him. It is he who "executes judgment, putting down one and lifting up another" (Psalm 75:7 ESV).

Consider the universe around us. Unlike the potter who takes something and reshapes it, God took nothing and created something. God created everything that exists. Prior to creation the universe was not a dark space. The universe did not exist. God even created the darkness. "I am the one who creates the light and makes the darkness" (Isaiah 45:7 NLT). John proclaimed, "You created everything, and it is for your pleasure that they exist and were created" (Revelation 4:11 NLT).

His knowledge about you is as complete as his knowledge about the universe. "Even before a word is on my tongue, behold, O LORD, you know it altogether. . . . Your eyes saw my unformed substance; in your book were written, every one of them, the days that were formed for me, when as yet there were none of them" (Psalm 139:4, 16 ESV).

> The veils that block your vision and mine do not block God's. Unspoken words are as if uttered. Unrevealed thoughts are as if proclaimed. Unoccurred moments are as if they were history.

He knows the future, the past, the hidden, and the untold. Nothing is concealed from God. He is all-powerful, all-knowing, and all-present.

 See the "holy otherness" of God? In Isaiah's encounter, those who see him most clearly regard him most highly. He is so holy that sinless seraphim cannot bear to look at him!

Isaiah could relate. When he sees the holiness of God, Isaiah does not boast or swagger. Instead, he falls on his face and begs for mercy. "Woe is me, for I am ruined! Because I am a man of unclean lips, and I live among a people of unclean lips; for my eyes have seen the King, the LORD of hosts" (Isaiah 6:5).

Emma Arthur encountered the holiness of God in a fresh way while helping build a house in Battle Creek, Michigan.

Emma Arthur
December 2004

I first heard about Habitat for Humanity when I was in my early teens, and I decided to apply to the Summer Youth Blitz (SYB) because I liked the challenge of a new experience. The mission of the SYB was to unite fourteen diverse teens from across the United States to work together for one common mission—to blitz build a house in two weeks. The challenge of the mission was to put aside our differences and work together.

Before my SYB experience, I was quick to judge others who were not like me. After working with the blitz crew, I further understood God's intention in making each of us unique. I also learned that in the uniqueness of our individuality, we all carry the presence of God.

My experience with SYB taught me that God's holiness is present daily, in heaven and earth. By humbling myself with those less fortunate, I testified that "It's not about me, it's about him."

One of my favorite Bible quotes is from First John: "Dear children, let us stop just saying we love each other; let us really show it by our actions" (1 John 3:18 NLT). In returning from my blitz build in Battle Creek, Michigan, I have

resolved to make that quote a motto for my life.
The things I do in my daily life are for him, and I
make an effort to see the face of God in others
each day. So many people in today's world "talk
the talk" and live a life of "me, me, me." By putting our love into our daily actions, we spread the
love of God to others and not just merely talk.
The actions that we express show that what we
do is not about us, but about him.[3]

One glimpse of God's glory, and Isaiah claimed citizen-
ship among the infected and diseased—the "unclean," a
term used to describe those with leprosy. The God-given
vision was not about Isaiah, however, but about God and
his glory. Isaiah gets the point. "It's not about me. It's all
about him."

One glimpse of God's glory in the faces of others who
were different from Emma, and she got the point too. It's not
about us. It's about him.

And God's mercy makes us holy. Look what happens next.

Then one of the seraphim flew to me with a
burning coal in his hand, which he had taken
from the altar with tongs. He touched my
mouth with it and said, "Behold, this has
touched your lips; and your iniquity is taken
away and your sin is forgiven." (Isaiah 6:6–7)

Isaiah makes no request. He asks for no grace. Indeed, he likely assumed mercy was impossible. But God, who is quick to pardon and full of mercy, purges Isaiah of his sin and redirects his life.

God asks for a spokesman. "Whom shall I send, and who will go for Us?" (Isaiah 6:8).

Isaiah's heart and hand shoot skyward. "Here am I. Send me!" (Isaiah 6:8). A glimpse of God's holiness and Isaiah had to speak. As if he'd seen what Moses had seen—God himself. Just a glimpse, but a God-glimpse nonetheless.

And Isaiah was different as a result.

And Emma Arthur was different as a result.

And with one glimpse of God's glory we will be different as well.

Holy different.

(41)

◐◒◓◑ *a thought question* ◐◒◓◑

If you had an encounter with the holy, holy, holy God, what do you think it would change about you?

Now *live* like you mean it.
Answer the questions on pages 147–148.

chapter 5

just a moment

September 11, 2001, was a moment in history that changed America. It opened our eyes to evils we hardly knew existed. It showcased the heroism of hundreds of "ordinary people." And it gave birth to new stereotypes and prejudices. One moment that changed so much.

For Tamara Shaya, standing against that prejudice was a moment-by-moment task. Tamara's parents were born in Baghdad, Iraq, even though they live in Cincinnati, Ohio. After 9/11 she faced teasing and stereotypes. "I could have become angry and bitter," she says. "But instead . . . I turned the other cheek. Instead of making a rude comeback, I simply walked away. I learned to be strong and to trust God for my protection." Tamara's choice to trust God during moments of trials will no doubt guide her as she follows her dream to become a missionary in Iraq.[1]

Think back before 9/11. Think back before people even counted time. Before "moments." Is that what life in the Garden was like for Adam and Eve? Before the couple swallowed the line of Satan and the fruit of the tree, no one printed calendars or wore watches or needed cemeteries. They lived in a time-free world. But in the moment it took to bite into the fruit, sin entered the world and, with it, time.

Our lives are a collection of moments, a measurable and countable supply, like change in a pocket. Your pocket may be full of decades, my pocket may be down to a few years, but everyone has a certain number of moments.

Everyone, that is, except God. As we list the mind-stretching claims of Christ, let's include this one near the top. "Before

Abraham was born, I am" (John 8:58). Jesus claimed to be God, the Eternal Being. He identified himself as "the High and Lofty One Who inhabits eternity" (Isaiah 57:15 NKJV).

Scripture broadcasts this attribute in surround-sound. God is "from everlasting" (Psalm 93:2 NKJV) and the "everlasting King" (Jeremiah 10:10 NKJV), "incorruptible" (Romans 1:23 NKJV), "who alone has immortality" (1 Timothy 6:16 NKJV). The heavens and the earth will perish, "but You [O God] are the same, and Your years will have no end" (Psalm 102:27 NKJV). You'll more quickly measure the salt of the ocean than measure the existence of God because "the number of His years is unsearchable" (Job 36:26).

Trace the tree back to a seed. Trace the dress back to a factory. Trace the baby back to a mommy. Trace God back to . . . to . . . to . . .

No one. Not even God made God. "From eternity I am He" (Isaiah 43:13). For that reason we have Jesus making statements such as, "Before Abraham was born, I am" (John 8:58). He didn't say, "Before Abraham was born, I *was*." God never says, "I was," because he still is. He is—right now—in the days of Abraham and in the end of time. He is eternal.

> **God** does not **live** in sequential moments, laid out on a **time** line, one following the **other**.

He does not live in sequential moments, laid out on a time line, one following the other. His world is one moment, or, better stated, momentless.

He doesn't view history as a progression of centuries but as a single photo. He captures your life, your entire life, in one glance. He sees your birth and burial in one frame. He knows

(45)

your beginning and your end, because he has neither.

Doesn't make sense, does it? Eternity makes no sense to us, the timebound. You might as well be handed a book written in Kanji (unless, of course, you are Japanese). You look at the characters, and all you see is zigzagged lines. You shake your head. This language finds no home in your mind.

But what if someone taught you how to read and write the language? Suppose a native speaker had the time and you had the will so that day by day the symbols that had meant nothing to you began to mean something?

> *Tucked **away** in each of us is a hunch that we were made for **forever** and a hope that the hunch is **true**.*

With God's help, the same is happening to you and me regarding eternity. He is teaching us the language. "He has also set eternity in their heart" (Ecclesiastes 3:11). Tucked away in each of us is a hunch that we were made for forever and a hope that the hunch is true.

But the idea of forever is hard to wrap our minds around. If grains of sand measured your time in heaven against your time on earth, how would they stack up? Heaven would be every grain of sand on every beach on earth, plus more. Earthly life, by contrast, would be one-hundredth of one grain of sand. Need a phrase to summarize the length of your life on earth? Try "a moment."

Wasn't this the phrase of choice for Paul? "Our light affliction, which is but *for a moment,* is working for us a far more exceeding and eternal weight of glory" (2 Corinthians 4:17 NKJV; emphasis mine).

What if we had a glimpse of the apostle as he wrote those words? By this time he had been "beaten times without number, often in danger of death. Five times," he writes, "I received from the Jews thirty-nine lashes. [In that day, forty lashes was considered a death sentence!] Three times I was beaten with rods, once I was stoned, three times I was shipwrecked, a night and a day I have spent in the deep" (2 Corinthians 11:23–25). He goes on to refer to life-threatening river trips, wilderness wanderings, and exposure to cold, attacks, hunger, and thirst. These, in Paul's words, are light afflictions to be endured for just a moment.

What if we took the same attitude toward life? What if we saw our tough times as a grain of sand scarcely worthy of contrast with the forever dunes?

The brevity of life grants power to abide, not an excuse to bail. Fleeting days don't justify fleeing problems. Fleeting days strengthen us to endure problems. Will your problems pass? No guarantee they will. Will your pain cease? Perhaps. Perhaps not. But heaven gives this promise: "our light affliction, which is but for a moment, is working for us a far more exceeding and eternal weight of glory" (2 Corinthians 4:17 NKJV).

> He **captures** your life, your entire life, in one **glance**.

Nineteen-year-old Peter Frost learned how to endure some tough moments because his goal far outweighed his struggles. He chose to walk the Appalachian Trail, which begins in Georgia and winds through fourteen eastern states before it ends in Maine—and he did it alone.

Greg Asimakoupoulos
Breakaway **magazine,**
August 2003

Ever since he was a little boy playing with his cousins in rural Illinois, Peter dreamed of adventure. He loved to spend hours hiking and swimming and constructing physical competitions to test his endurance. When he entered Wheaton Academy, he jumped at the opportunity to spend his summers going on missions trips. They included evangelistic adventures to Alaska, Arizona, Guatemala, and the Dominican Republic.

Without admitting it to anyone, Peter began to plan to walk the Appalachian Trail the summer after his freshman year at Wheaton College. He talked to one of the leaders from his missions trips for some trusted advice. "He thought it was a great goal, but he didn't think a three-month summer vacation was enough time to do it," Peter says with a smile. "He told me that from everything he'd read, it takes the average person a minimum of six months to complete the Appalachian Trail. But as I continued to press him, he eventually backed off and said I just might be the one who could pull it off."

Peter began a five-month program of cardio-vascular and strength conditioning. In addition to weight training and a daily regimen of calisthenics, Peter came up with his own approach to get his legs in shape. "I crammed my backpack full of textbooks and blankets and then wore it while clocking miles on the StairMaster in the weight room," Peter says. "I got some pretty interesting looks. But I didn't mind. I knew what my goal was." He also talked his friend John into being a human backpack. Carrying his 175-pound classmate piggyback, Peter proceeded to climb the eight floors of his dorm several times a week.

Finally, with his family and church friends praying for his health and safety, Peter waved good-bye to his dad and brother and stepped off at the trailhead in Springer Mountain, Georgia, on May 12, 2002.

By day eight of his adventure, Peter was blindsided by homesickness and blisters on his feet the size of his thumbs. On day nine Peter found a pay phone and called Doug Franklin, who had coordinated the missions trips he had been on in high school. "Doug could hear my voice shaking," Peter says. "He could tell I needed encouragement. He told me a couple things that really buoyed my spirits. First he said that on a long trip you can't just focus on the ultimate destination. Instead, you have to focus on getting through each day. He also said I had to find something every day to make the trek special.

"The Lord knew I needed that shot in the arm," Peter says. "For the next month I was able to maintain my momentum and keep a positive attitude. Chewing on Psalm 119 every morning and devouring letters from home helped me keep my focus. But I gotta tell you—although I relied on Snickers bars to give me quick energy, after two hundred of them, they grew pretty sickening!"

On day thirty-eight Peter hit another low. Having logged 213 miles on his second pair of hiking boots in eight days, his feet were covered with open sores. Every step was excruciatingly painful. But once again the Lord knew just what Peter needed. That night at the nearest shelter he met a middle-aged man who expressed concern about Peter's condition. "His name was Rich," Peter recalls. "He told me he used to be a Navy Seal. What was even cooler was the fact that he was a Christian. He spent the next day hiking with me and encouraging me to stick with it. He told me he believed in me."

By the time Peter reached the White Mountains in New Hampshire, he felt like he wasn't making enough progress. When he reached an elaborate wilderness lodge called Mizpah Hut, it seemed part of God's plan. "After being alone for nearly three months, I was beginning to doubt my abilities to keep going. But the Lord knew what I needed, and once again He provided me with the encouragement—and hot shower—I needed."

It was at the wilderness lodge that Peter met up with another nineteen-year-old on the trail. Although his name was Ryan, the boy had adopted "Two Step" as his trail name. Since most of the hikers Peter had met on the trail were retirement age or in their late twenties, he was curious about what had triggered Two Step to tackle the A.T. The story the boy told was more than Peter had bargained for.

"Two Step told me he was only walking the second half of the trail," Peter recalls. "His older brother had hiked the first half the summer before. The brother had hoped to do the second half the next summer but had been tragically killed in a car accident that winter. Two Step was finishing what his brother had wanted to. He was walking to the end of the trail in honor of his brother. That's what his trail name meant."

Peter invited his new friend to hike with him for the final fifteen days of the trek, and Two Step accepted. It was during this last leg of the journey that Peter received news from home that a classmate at Wheaton College had been killed in a car accident.

"It was really a God thing," Peter admits. "Just think of it. Here I am hiking with a guy my age whose brother had died in a car accident six months earlier, and I get word that a friend two doors down on my floor just died the same way. It opened a door for me to talk with Two Step about what it means to have a relationship with Jesus. We talked about heaven and hell and how it's possible to be certain of where you will go when you die."

On August 23, knowing the end was in sight, Peter talked Two Steps into hiking all night by flashlight. When dawn broke the next morning, they had gone fifty-two miles in one day and night to reach the base of Mount Katahdin, Maine. There Peter's mom joined them for the final ten miles of the trail up Katahdin.

"I can't really describe all that I was feeling when I reached the end of the trail," Peter says with a grin. "Mostly it was exhaustion. But there was a whole lot more. For one thing I was overwhelmed with how much being a Christian is like a three-month hike. In order to reach the finish line you have to focus on following Jesus a day at a time. I guess maybe that's why they call it 'walking with the Lord.'"[2]

"Light afflictions" versus the "weight of glory," says the apostle Paul.

The words "weight of glory" remind me of the blindfolded lady of justice. She holds a scale with two pans, one on either

◀◆▼▶ *Chapter 14* ◀◆▼▶
upward thinking

In the space below, write a letter to God.
Pour out your heart. Confess your failures, and
embrace his forgiveness. Admit your deepest
spiritual longings, and call upon his infinite power.
Describe the kind of God-centered life you'd like to
have, and claim the certain promises of Christ.

_____

_____

_____

_____

_____

_____

_____

_____

_____

_____

_____

_____

_____

_____

How can you use your accomplishments to talk about God in a way that doesn't sound fake?

chapter 6

his unchanging hand

1966. Lyndon Johnson was president.

The best known Bush was the one that spoke to Moses. Vietnam rumbled. Hippies rocked. Woodstock was a dairy farm, and the Lucados were moving into a new home.

LBJ soon moved back to Texas, and the Bushes moved to Washington. Vietnam, hippies, and Woodstock faded like tie-dyed T-shirts, but the Lucado family stayed in that yellow-brick house. For thirty-five years we stayed.

> *Ever feel like screaming, "Stop! **No more change!**"*

The Beatles came and went. The economy rose and fell and rose again. Much changed, but there was always a Lucado living in the three-bedroom house just off Avenue G.

Until today. As I write, movers load three decades of family life into a truck. The mailman is peeling "Lucado" off the mailbox and stenciling on "Hernandez."

The vacating was bound to happen. It had to happen. But it's hard to see it happen. Change, like taxes, is necessary but unwelcome.

Change? a few of you are thinking. *You want to talk about change? Let me tell you about change . . .*

Let me tell you about my changing body—It seems every week my feet are bigger and my jeans shorter.

My changing family—My mom and dad don't get along, and I'm afraid they're about to split up.

My changing friends—Some of my friends are experimenting with drugs and messing up their lives.

Change. Had more than your share? Wish you could freeze-frame the video of your world? Ever feel like screaming, "Stop! No more change!"?

Save your breath. If you're looking for a place with no change, try a soda machine. With life comes change.

With change comes fear, insecurity, sorrow, stress. So what do you do? Hibernate? Take no chances for fear of failing? Give no love for fear of losing? Some decide it is too risky. They hold back.

A better idea is to look up. Set your bearings on the one and only North Star in the universe—God. For though life changes, he never does. Scripture makes pupil-popping claims about his permanence.

Consider his strength. Unending. According to Paul, God's power lasts forever (Romans 1:20). His strength never diminishes. Yours and mine will and has. Our energy ebbs and flows more than the Mississippi River. You aren't as alert in the morning as in the evening. You won't run as fast when you are eighty as when you are twenty. Even the strongest among us must eventually rest. Lance Armstrong can maintain a bike speed of 32 mph for a solid hour. Healthy college males last forty-five seconds at that pace. I'd make thirty before wanting to throw up. Armstrong lives up to the last half of his last name. He is strong. But at some point he must rest. His head seeks the pillow, and his body seeks sleep.[1]

Paul Hamm—now he's strong. His veins burst through his biceps, his forearms are massive, and his shoulders are broad. Michigan coach Kurt Golder said, "Gymnasts get stronger than most of the other athletes that are in the weight room.

When I was coaching in high school, I had a kid in gymnastics for two years who weighed 114 pounds. The first time he touched the bench press, he could do 235 pounds. He was outbenching most of the football players."[2] A gymnast is strong, but he won't be strong forever.

God will. The words "I'm feeling strong today" he has never said. He feels equally strong every day.

> Certainly the **"truth"** of the world wavers. **Opinions** change at the speed of fashion **trends**.

Daniel calls him "the living God, enduring forever" (Daniel 6:26 ESV). The psalmist tells him, "I will sing of your strength. . . . For you have been to me a fortress and a refuge in the day of my distress. O my Strength, I will sing praises to you, for you, O God, are my fortress, the God who shows me steadfast love" (Psalm 59:16–17 ESV).

Think about it. God never pauses to eat or asks the angels to cover for him while he naps. He never signals a time-out or puts the prayer requests from Russia on hold while he handles South Africa. He "never tires and never sleeps" (Psalm 121:4 NLT). Need a strong hand to hold? You'll always find one in his. His strength never changes.

Need unchanging truth to trust? Try God's. His truth never wavers.

Wish that we could say the same. Certainly the "truth" of the world wavers. Opinions change at the speed of fashion trends.

Good to know God's opinions don't. His view of right and wrong is the same with you and me as it was with Adam and Eve. "The word of our God shall stand for ever" (Isaiah 40:8

KJV). "For ever, O LORD, thy word is settled in heaven. . . . All thy commandments are truth. . . . Thou hast founded them for ever" (Psalm 119:89, 151–152 KJV).

Your outlook may change. My convictions may sway, but "the Scripture cannot be broken" (John 10:35 NKJV). And since it can't, since his truth will not waver, God's ways will never alter.

He will always hate sin and love sinners, despise the proud and lift up the humble. He will always convict the evildoer and comfort the heavy-hearted. He never changes direction midstream, revises the course midway home, or amends the heavenly Constitution. God will always be the same.

No one else will. Friends call you today and talk about you tomorrow. Classmates applaud you when you drive a classic and dismiss you when you drive a dud. People make promises one day and break them the next. Not God. God is "always the same" (Psalm 102:27 NLT). With him "there is no variation or shadow due to change" (James 1:17 ESV).

Catch God in a bad mood? Won't happen. Fear exhausting his grace? A sardine will swallow the Atlantic first. Think he's given up

> Catch God in a **bad** mood? **Won't** happen.

on you? Wrong. Did he not make a promise to you? "God is not a human being, and he will not lie. He is not a human, and he does not change his mind. What he says he will do, he does. What he promises, he makes come true" (Numbers 23:19 NCV). He's never sullen or sour, sulking or stressed. His strength, truth, ways, and love never change. He is "the same yesterday and today and forever" (Hebrews 13:8 ESV). And because he is, the Lord "will be the stability of your times" (Isaiah 33:6 NKJV).

Joseph Rojas thought God—if there was a God—had given up on him.

Joseph Rojas
December 2003

My father left when I was around three years old, and my only memories of him were his beating my mother bloody. I grew up dreaming of having a father. I never really fit in with the other kids. I was the fat kid who never got picked for any teams. As a teen I started using drugs to take my pain away. soon I started selling drugs and getting in trouble with the law. I ended up in jail a couple of times and finally got charged with my first felony. I was not a Christian. I didn't care whether or not there was a God. Even if there was a God, why would he want a worthless drug addict like me? By this time I had a $400 a day cocaine addiction, and I was a two-time felon with no hope for the future. I hated myself, and not a day went by that I didn't think about blowing my brains out.

After stealing from my own mother to get high, I decided to take my life and began to try to overdose on cocaine. My mother walked in unexpectedly and saw me overdose. She was crying out to God and called the paramedics. While I was in the ambulance, I felt the power of God! I

called out to Jesus to save my life, and for the first time, I felt like I got picked!

I have given everything I am to Christ, and he has taken me places I never even dreamed were possible. I now sing in a Christian band, Seventh Day Slumber, to tell others about God's faithfulness and unchanging love. I have been nominated for Dove Awards, have had #1 songs on the radio, and have led over nineteen thousand young people to Christ! I am crazy enough to believe the scripture that I can do all things through Christ who strengthens me! I am not perfect; I still make mistakes, and I still sometimes feel down, but now I have a place that I can go for strength, and that place is Jesus Christ![3]

God had a plan, an eternal plan for Joseph Rajas. And even when Joseph didn't believe in him and rejected him—as Joseph did at first—God's plans do not change. Why? Because God makes his plans in complete knowledge of the past, the present, and the future. Forget hopeful forecasting. He declares "the end from the beginning" (Isaiah 46:10). Nothing takes him by surprise. "The plans of the LORD stand firm forever" (Psalm 33:11 NIV).

> **Nothing** takes him by **surprise**.

The Cross will not lose its power. The blood of Christ will not fade in strength. God will never return to the

drawing board. "What He does in time He planned from eternity. And all that He planned in eternity He carries out in time."[4]

"The LORD Almighty has spoken—who can change his plans? When his hand moves, who can stop him?" (Isaiah 14:27 NLT). God never changes. Everyone else does. Everything else will.

In the hours I prepared this message, the movers all but emptied the Lucado house. Christmas meals, dinner-table laughter, good-night hugs for my clan under that roof—all past tense. Yet another constant becomes a transient. What changes are you facing?

Cemeteries interrupt the finest families.

Circumstances alter the best plans.

Disease attacks the strongest bodies.

With life comes change.

But with change comes the reassuring appreciation of heaven's permanence. His "firm foundation stands" (2 Timothy 2:19 ESV). His house will stand forever.

(62)

◁△▽▷ *a thought question* ◁△▽▷

*Can you face the changes in your life
holding firmly to the unchanging hand of God?*

Now *live* like you mean it.
Answer the questions on pages 151-152.

chapter 7

God's great love

Several hundred feet beneath my chair is a lake, an underground cavern of crystalline water known as the Edwards Aquifer. We South Texans know much about this aquifer. We know its length (175 miles). We know its layout (west to east except under San Antonio, where it runs north to south). We know the water is pure. Fresh. It irrigates farms and waters lawns and fills pools and quenches thirst. We know much about the aquifer.

> We know the **impact** of God's **love**. But the volume? No person has **ever** measured it.

But for all the facts we do know, there is an essential one we don't. We don't know its size. The depth of the cavern? A mystery. Number of gallons? Unmeasured. No one knows the amount of water the aquifer contains.

Watch the nightly weather report, and you'd think otherwise. Meteorologists give regular updates on the aquifer level. You get the impression that the amount of water is calculated. "The truth is," a friend told me, "no one knows how much water is down there."

64

Remarkable. We use it, depend upon it, would perish without it . . . but measure it? We can't.

Bring to mind another unmeasured pool? It might. Not a pool of water but a pool of love. God's love. Immerse a life in God's love, and watch it emerge cleansed and changed. We know the impact of God's love.

But the volume? No person has ever measured it.

Who has measured the depth of God's love? Only God has. "Want to see the size of my love?" he invites. "Ascend the winding path outside of Jerusalem. Follow the dots of bloody

dirt until you crest the hill. Before looking up, pause and hear me whisper, 'This is how much I love you.'"

Condemned to die by crucifixion. Whip-ripped muscles drape his back. Blood streams down his face. His eyes and lips are swollen shut. Pain rages at wildfire intensity. As he sinks to relieve the agony of his legs, his airway closes. At the edge of suffocation, he shoves pierced muscles against the spike and inches up the cross. He does this for hours. Painfully up and down until his strength and our doubts are gone.

> **Does God *love* you? Look at the *cross*, and you find your *answer*.**

(65)

Does God love you? Look at the cross, and you find your answer.

How does one understand such love? Surprisingly, Amy Morsch found a piece of the answer in the Home for Dying Destitutes.

Amy Morsch, as told to Dean Nelson
Christianity Today
February 1999

There's no way you can properly prepare for Calcutta. Even the billboard on the highway going into the city makes you wonder what you've gotten yourself into. It says, "Welcome to Calcutta—a City of Filth, Hunger, Warmth, Smiles and Joy!"

I thought I was ready when I left for India. I was a college student traveling with a group of volunteers as part of a twelve-million-dollar airlift organized by Heart to Heart International, a Christian ministry founded by my dad.

But when we got to Calcutta, I was immediately overwhelmed. I felt a sense of hopelessness as I looked at the skin-and-bones children, the human waste in the streets, the flies, the women sitting in front of mounds of animal waste, making patties with their bare hands and baking them over open fires to sell as fuel. And the sights were nothing compared to the smell of the city—a mixture of death, feces, and rotten food.

During our time in Calcutta, we talked with people on the streets and visited orphanages and hospitals. But my most meaningful experience happened at a place called the Home for Dying Destitutes—a place for dying people who have nowhere else to go.

One of the workers in the home suggested that I help feed the lady in cot 17—a lady who was too weak to feed herself. She weighed about seventy pounds, had three teeth and paper-thin skin. The diaper she wore needed changing, and she babbled constantly in a language I couldn't understand. I would like to tell you that my first thought was, *Of course I'll help her—she's one of God's children just like I am.* But it wasn't. My

first response was that this work was too far below me, too gross. But there was a sign on the wall that said, "Do small things with great love." It seemed to say to me, "It's not what you do, or how much you do; what matters is the love you put in the doing."

So I went to the woman in cot 17 and fed her small bites of rice, curry, and fish. She ate a little, but what she wanted most was for me to sit so close to her that we were touching, as if she craved the touch of another human being more than she craved food. The longer I looked at her, the more I realized this wasn't just a meal that was happening. Finally, as I held a cup of water to her lips, she pointed at her heart, then pointed at me.

In that very moment I experienced a whole new kind of love, the kind I think God must feel for us. I knew I would do anything for this woman. I said, "I love you" to her, and as soon as I did, tears came pouring out of my eyes. When the words left my mouth, I felt that I experienced God's love for me, too. I have done nothing to deserve his love, and yet it overwhelms me. As he showed in the life of Jesus, God has said, "I will do anything for you."

I left the home thinking, *God chooses to come at the weirdest moments.* Later I realized that it wasn't such a weird moment. It was the Thursday before Easter—the night Jesus washed his disciples' feet.

A few weeks later, when I got back to my comfortable room in my comfortable house in Kansas, I realized my experience in Calcutta wasn't one of those emotional highs that go away after a few weeks. The lady in cot 17—I never did get her name—is like an anchor in my mind. Experiencing God's love through her has changed the way I work as a resident assistant in my college dormitory. Sometimes, as I am dealing with a situation in the dorm and I really want to be doing something else, I realize that in those moments, the girls in my dorm are the "least of these" Jesus talks about in Matthew 25:40. I need to treat them the way I would treat Jesus if he were right in front of me. My experience in Calcutta sits at the front of my brain and affects virtually every decision I make.

Going to Calcutta showed me that my whole life boils down to Jesus's words, "Love one another." We are on this earth to show God's love. And we don't have to go to Calcutta to do it. As the sign in the Home for the Dying Destitutes showed me, it's not how much you do, it's how much love you put into what you do.[1]

God the Son died for the woman in cot 17. And God the Son died for you. Who could have imagined such a gift?

God could have given his children a great idea or a lyrical message or an endless song . . . but he gave himself. "[God the

Son] loved us and gave himself up for us as a fragrant offering and sacrifice to God" (Ephesians 5:2 NIV). What species of devotion is this? Find the answer under the category "unfailing." The holiness of God demanded a sinless sacrifice, and the only sinless sacrifice was God the Son. And since God's love never fails to pay the price, he did. God loves you with an unfailing love.

But how does God's love square with the theme of this book? After all, "It's not about me." If it's not about me, does God care about me? God's priority is his glory. He occupies center stage; I carry props. He's the message; I'm but a word. Is this love?

No doubt. Do you really want the world to revolve around you? If it's all about you, then it's all up to you. Your Father rescues you from

> *If it's all **about** you, then it's all **up** to you.*

such a burden. While you are valuable, you aren't essential. You're important but not indispensable.

Still don't think that's good news?

Perhaps Will's experience will help explain.

Although the Rio Grande is the only thing that separates Juárez, Mexico, from El Paso, Texas, the two are literally worlds apart. In Mexico minimum wage hovers around $5.00 a day. With so many families living in extreme poverty and inadequate housing, the pastors have found that these physical limitations hamper their ability to impress people that there is a God who loves them enough to take care of their needs. Casas por Cristo-"Houses Because of Christ"—was founded not

only to take care of this physical need but to address spiritual needs as well. After leading a team to build homes in Mexico, Will Forsythe, a teenager from Colorado, said, "The highlight of my trip was seeing God take control of the trip even though I was the leader."[2]

God knows your limitations. He's well aware of your weaknesses. That's why the world doesn't rely on you. God loves you too much to say it's all about you. We don't know what it takes to run the world, and wise are we who leave the work to his hands.

> To say "It's not about you" is not to say you aren't loved; quite the contrary. It's because God loves you that it's not about you.

And, oh, what a love this is. It's "too wonderful to be measured" (Ephesians 3:19 CEV). But though we cannot measure it, may I urge you to trust it? Some of you are so hungry for such love. Those who should have loved you didn't. Those who could have loved you wouldn't. And you are left with the question, "Does anybody love me?"

Please listen to heaven's answer. As you ponder Jesus on the cross, hear God assure, "I do."

Someday someone will likely find the limits of the South Texas aquifer. A robotic submarine, even a diver, will descend through the water until it hits solid ground. "We've plumbed the depths," newspapers will announce. Will someone say the same of God's love? No. When it comes to water, we'll find the limit. But when it comes to his love, we never will.

◊◊◊◊ *a thought question* ◊◊◊◊

Name one way it takes weight off your shoulders to admit that the world doesn't revolve around you.

Now live like you mean it.
Answer the questions on pages 153–154.

part two

God-promoting

chapter 8

God's mirrors

G. R. Tweed looked across the Pacific waters at the American ship on the horizon. Brushing the jungle sweat from his eyes, the young naval officer swallowed deeply and made his decision. This could be his only chance for escape.

Tweed had been hiding on Guam for nearly three years. When the Japanese occupied the island in 1941, he ducked into the thick tropical brush. Survival hadn't been easy, but he preferred the swamp to a POW camp.

Late in the day July 10, 1944, he spotted the friendly vessel. He scurried up a hill and positioned himself on a cliff. He reached into his pack and pulled out a small mirror. At 6:20 p.m., he began sending signals. Holding the edge of the mirror in his fingers, he tilted it back and forth, bouncing the sunrays in the direction of the boat. Three short flashes. Three long. Three short again. Dot-dot-dot. Dash-dash-dash. Dot-dot-dot. SOS.

The signal caught the eye of a sailor on board the USS *McCall.* A rescue party boarded a motorized dinghy and slipped into the cove past the coastal guns. Tweed was rescued.[1]

He was glad to have that mirror, glad he knew how to use it, and glad that the mirror cooperated. Suppose it hadn't. (Prepare yourself for a crazy thought.) Suppose the mirror had resisted, pushed its own agenda. Rather than reflect a message from the sun, suppose it had opted to send its own. After all, three years of isolation would leave one starved for attention. Rather than sending an SOS, the mirror could have sent an LAM. "Look at me."

An egotistical mirror?

The only crazier thought would be an insecure mirror. *What if I blow it? What if I send a dash when I'm supposed to send a dot? Besides, have you seen the blemishes on my surface?* Self-doubt could paralyze a mirror.

So could self-pity. *Been crammed down in that pack, lugged through jungles, and now, all of a sudden expected to face the bright sun and perform a crucial service. No way. Staying in the pack. Not getting any reflection out of me.*

Good thing Tweed's mirror didn't have a mind of its own.

But God's mirrors? Unfortunately we do.

We are his mirrors, you know. Reduce the human job description down to one phrase, and this is it: reflect God's glory. As Paul wrote: "And we, with our unveiled faces reflecting like mirrors the brightness of the Lord, all grow brighter and brighter as we are turned into the image that we reflect; this is the work of the Lord who is Spirit" (2 Corinthians 3:18 JB).

Perhaps you have read this verse in a different translation, such as the New American Standard Bible:

> **We are his mirrors.**

"But we all, with unveiled face, *beholding as in a mirror* the glory of the Lord, are being transformed into the same image from glory to glory, just as from the Lord, the Spirit" (emphasis mine).

One translation says, "*beholding* as in a mirror"; another says, "*reflecting* like mirrors." Which is accurate?

Actually both. The Greek verb *katoptrizo* can be translated either way. Translators are in both camps.

But which meaning did Paul intend? In the context of the

passage, Paul paralleled the Christian experience to the Mount Sinai experience of Moses. After Moses *beheld* the glory of God, his face *reflected* the glory of God. His face was so dazzling white that the "people of Israel could no more look right at him than stare into the sun" (2 Corinthians 3:7 MSG).

Upon beholding God, Moses could not help but reflect God. *The brightness he saw was the brightness he became.* Beholding led to becoming. Becoming led to reflecting. Perhaps the answer to the translation question, then, is yes.

Did Paul mean "*beholding* as in a mirror"? Yes.

Did Paul mean "*reflecting* like mirrors"? Yes.

Could it be that the Holy Spirit intentionally selected a verb that would remind us to do both? To behold God so intently that we can't help but reflect him?

What does it mean to behold your face in a mirror? A quick glance? A casual look? No. To behold is to study, to stare, to contemplate. Beholding God's glory, then, is no side look or occasional glance; this beholding is a serious pondering.

78

And as we behold his glory, dare we pray that we, like Moses, will reflect it? Dare we hope to be mirrors in the hands of God, the reflection of the light of God? This is the call.

"Whatever you do, do all to the glory of God" (1 Corinthians 10:31 NKJV).

Whatever? Whatever.

Whether serving at school, participating in sports, creating music, working in a garden, volunteering in community projects, or going on a mission trip.

Lancaster New Era
Lancaster Catholic High School
October 5, 2002

Paul F. Squierdo marches to the beat of his own snare drum. The Lancaster Catholic High School senior keeps the beat with this instrument in the Crusaders Marching Band, which is just one outlet for his love of percussion. He plays a variety of percussion instruments—from congas to mallets to the drum set—in the school's concert band, jazz band, and percussion ensemble.

As the band's student director, Paul serves as a liaison between band members and staff. He also is section leader for the drum line. And as a member of the school's Young Apostles group, he plays drums for school Masses and student retreats and with the youth group band at his church, St. James Catholic in Lititz, Pennsylvania.

Despite his love for drums, Paul isn't planning on a musical career. Rather, he is interested in the field of landscape architecture. "I've been brought up in the outdoors," says the fly fisherman and Eagle Scout, whose project was restoring nature trails and building a retaining wall at the Millport Conservancy. He also has gotten his hands dirty gardening for neighbors.

In school, Paul plays on the baseball team,

and as a student ambassador, he welcomes visitors to the school during various events. He is also president of the Respect Life Club, which speaks out against abortion, capital punishment, and euthanasia by participating in such events as the March for Life in Washington, D.C. As a Catholic, he says, "We believe in letting God be the judge of who can stay and who can go."

The group also does social outreach projects, such as food and clothing drives, often in conjunction with the Young Apostles and the National Honor Society, of which he also is a member.

In July, Paul went with forty other Young Apostles members on a missions trip to Nashville to be part of the Catholic HEART Workcamp with students from other parts of the country. Paul's group assisted with tasks at an adult day-care center.

Such volunteer work, he says, is "a reflection of what my religion is all about—reaching out to others. It's an extension of my faith. It's a way I can live it out."[2]

We become reflectors of God's glory when the things we do highlight him.

Let your message reflect his glory. "Let your light shine before

men, that they may see your good deeds and praise your Father in heaven" (Matthew 5:16 NIV).

Let your salvation reflect God's glory. "Having believed, you were marked in him with a seal, the promised Holy Spirit, who is a deposit guaranteeing our inheritance until the redemption of those who are God's possession—to the praise of his glory" (Ephesians 1:13–14 NIV).

> We become **reflectors** of God's **glory** when the things we do highlight **him**.

(81)

Let your body reflect God's glory. "You are not your own. . . . Glorify God in your body" (1 Corinthians 6:19–20).

Your struggles. "These sufferings of ours are for your benefit. And the more of you who are won to Christ, the more there are to thank him for his great kindness, and the more the Lord is glorified" (2 Corinthians 4:15 TLB; see also John 11:4).

Your success honors God. "Honor the LORD with your wealth" (Proverbs 3:9 NIV). "Riches and honor come from you" (1 Chronicles 29:12 NCV). "God . . . is giving you power to make wealth" (Deuteronomy 8:18).

> Your message, your salvation, your body, your struggles, your success—all can proclaim God's glory.

"Whatever you do in word or deed, do all in the name of the Lord Jesus, giving thanks through Him to God the Father" (Colossians 3:17).

That's Tricia's goal. During her senior year at Fountain Valley High School, in California, Tricia spent Wednesday afternoons leading ten other volunteers as

they did craft projects, read stories, and played games with twenty children living at Thomas House, a temporary shelter for homeless families. Tricia says, "A lot of people think God has forgotten the poor. But God uses people like me and other volunteers to reach out to those in need."[3]

Both Tricia and Paul figured out the difference between God's place in life and our place.

He's the source; we are the glass. He's the light; we are the mirrors. He sends the message; we mirror it. We rest in his pack awaiting his call. And when placed in his hands, we do his work. It's not about us; it's all about him.

Mr. Tweed's use of a mirror led to a rescue.

May God use us to rescue millions more.

◁◁◁◁ *a thought question* ◁◁◁◁

What part of your daily life could you start using to reflect God's glory?

**Now *live* like you mean it.
Answer the questions on pages 155–156.**

chapter 9

my message is about him

Behind him, a trail of tracks.

Beneath him, a pounding stallion.

Before him, miles of trail to cover.

Within him, rock-hard resolve.

Squinty eyed. Firm jawed. Tough as nails. Pony Express riders had one assignment . . . deliver the message safely and quickly. They seized every advantage: the shortest route, the fastest horse, the lightest saddle. Even the lightest lunchbox.

> *Paul existed to deliver the **message**. How people remembered him was **secondary**.*

Only the sturdy were hired. Could they handle the horses? The heat? Could they outrun robbers and outlast blizzards? The young and the orphans were preferred. Those selected were given $125 a month (a good salary in 1860), a Colt revolver, a lightweight rifle, a bright red shirt, blue trousers, and eight hours to cover eighty miles, six days a week.

Hard work and high pay. But the message was worth it.[1]

The apostle Paul would have loved the Pony Express. For he, like the riders, had been entrusted with a message.

"I have a duty to all people," Paul told the Roman church (Romans 1:14 NCV). He had something for them—a message. He'd been entrusted as a Pony Express courier with a divine message, the gospel. Nothing mattered more to Paul than the gospel. "I am not ashamed of the gospel," he wrote next, "because it is the power of God for the salvation of everyone who believes" (Romans 1:16 NIV).

Paul existed to deliver the message. How people remembered

him was secondary. (Else why would he introduce himself as a slave? [Romans 1:1 NLT]). How people remembered Christ was primary. Paul's message was not about himself. His message was all about Christ.

How difficult for us to maintain this focus. Don't we tend to tinker with the message? Aren't we prone to insert lines that serve our own purposes?

A young guide in the art museum was. One sentence summarized his job: lead people to the paintings, answer their questions, and step out of the way. Initially he succeeded. He walked the clients to the framed treasures, identified the artists, and stepped out of view.

"This is a Monet," he would say and move back as people oohed and aahed and asked a question or two. When they were ready, he would lead them to the next masterpiece and repeat the sequence. "This is the work of Rembrandt." He stepped back; they leaned in. He stood; they stared.

Simple job. Delightful job. He took great pride in his work.

Too much pride, one might say. For in a short time, he forgot his role. He began thinking the people had come to see him. Rather than step away from the work of art, he lingered near it. As they oohed and aahed, he smiled. "Glad you like it," he replied, chest lifting, face blushing. He even responded with an occasional "thank you," taking credit for work he didn't do.

Visitors disregarded his comments. But they couldn't dismiss his movements. Lingering near a painting was no longer sufficient for the guide. Little by little he inched toward it. Initially extending his arm over the frame, then his torso over

part of the canvas. Finally his body blocked the entire piece. People could see him but not the art. The very work he was sent to reveal he began to conceal.

That's when his Superior intervened. "This job isn't about you, Max. Don't obscure my masterpieces."

How many times has he had to remind me? The very first time I was called to display a painting, I was tempted to eclipse it.

The request came when I was twenty. "Can you address our church youth group?" We aren't talking citywide crusade here. Think more in terms of a dozen kids around a West Texas campfire. I was new to the faith, hence new to the power of the faith. I told my story, and, lo and behold, they listened! One even approached me afterward and said something like, "That moved me, Max." My chest lifted, and my feet shifted just a step in the direction of the painting.

> "What are **people** thinking of **you**?"

God has been nudging me back ever since.

Some of you don't relate. The limelight never woos you. You and John the Baptist sing the same tune: "He must become greater and greater, and I must become less and less" (John 3:30 NLT). God bless you. You might pray for the rest of us. We applause-aholics have done it all: dropped names, dressed up to look classy, dressed down to look cool, taken credit for things we haven't done. For the life of me, I believe Satan trains battalions of demons to whisper one question in our ears: "What are people thinking of you?"

A deadly query. What they think of us matters not. What

they think of God matters all. God will not share his glory with another (Isaiah 42:8). Next time you need a nudge away from the spotlight, remember: *you are simply one step in a process, an unimportant step at that.*

Don't agree? Take it up with the apostle. "So the one who plants *is not important,* and the one who waters *is not important.* Only God, who makes things grow, is important" (1 Corinthians 3:7 NCV; emphasis mine).

Remember the other messengers God has used?

A donkey to speak to Balaam (Numbers 22:28).

A staff-turned-snake to stir Pharaoh (Exodus 7:10).

He even used a big fish to make a point to the prophet Jonah (Jonah 1:1–17).

And he is now using sixteen-year-old Austin-Nichole's television program.

AmazingKids!
March 2003

Austin-Nichole Zachrich is a typical teenager, by most accounts. A resident in the small rural community of Defiance, Ohio, Austin-Nichole loves to hang out and go to the movies or play miniature golf with her friends. She enjoys singing and performing in plays and musicals. She also just happens to produce and host her own television program on several access cable stations.

Austin-Nichole says, "The show is positive, comical, and upbeat! We talk about topics that kids deal with every day and bring them current events, trivia, cool Web sites to check out, movie rental suggestions, crafts, and snack ideas. And we bring all this in a fun, entertaining way. We encourage our viewers to write in and share their thoughts and ideas. Occasionally kids write in and ask us for advice. We are not professionals by any means, but we have a segment known as "In Da Houze" for peer-to-peer questions and answers and try to help out!

"On a serious note, we always encourage kids to be involved in the world around them, so we share clubs and organizations that kids can get involved in. There are so many great ways for us to make a difference. I know firsthand, as volunteers run this show!

"We are always looking for kids who are doing something positive to impact our world. My main focus is positive messages from the media for today's youth. We learn by example, and I want to bring stories that inspire and make a difference in our world."

The topics that Austin-Nichole and her volunteers cover are varied: kids doing things that make you say wow!, sports, acting, diet and exercise for teens, recipes, crafts, magicians, volunteer organizations, academics, homework

helpers, art, musicians, bands, fashion, dating ideas, self-defense, amazing pets, overcoming obstacles, skin care, decorating for teens, and keeping organized. She also includes a segment entitled Angelic Thoughts, which brings "positive quotes in a heavenly fashion to the audience."

Austin-Nichole says, "I want to thank God for what he has made me so far and for the work he has yet to do."[2]

A modern-day Pony Express rider. A messenger of help and encouragement. An ambassador of inspiration. But Austin-Nichole knows who deserves the credit.

God doesn't need you and me to do his work. We are expedient messengers, ambassadors by his kindness, not by our cleverness.

It's not about us, and it angers him when we think it is. Jesus has a stern warning for gallery guides who eclipse his work.

> When you do something for someone else, don't call attention to yourself. You've seen them in action, I'm sure—"playactors" I call them—treating prayer meeting and street corner alike as a stage, acting compassionate as long as someone is watching, playing to the crowds. They get applause, true, but that's all they get. (Matthew 6:2 MSG)

Pony Express riders didn't take credit for kind letters.

Gallery guides don't deserve applause for great art.

> And we who are entrusted with the gospel dare not seek applause but better deflect applause. For our message is about Someone else.

A European village priest in medieval times once gathered his church for a special service. "Come tonight," he told them, "for a special sermon on Jesus." And they did. They came. To their surprise, however, no candles illuminated the sanctuary. They groped their way to the pews and took their seats. The priest was nowhere to be seen. But soon he was heard walking through the church toward the front. When he reached the crucifix that hung on the wall, he lit a candle. Saying nothing, he illuminated the pierced feet of Christ, then the side, then one hand, and then the other. Lifting the candle, he shed light on the blood-masked face and the crown of thorns. With a puff, he blew out the candle and dismissed the church.[3]

May we do nothing more.

May we do nothing less.

◁△▽▷ ***a thought question*** ◁△▽▷

*Without speaking a word, how could you be a
messenger this week of the good news of Jesus?*

*Now **live** like you mean it.
Answer the questions on pages 157–158.*

chapter 10

my salvation is about him

Meet Laura Hippensteel, a girl who can run like the wind, turn on a fastball, and cover every inch of center field. In addition, the senior at Centennial High in Franklin, Tennessee, carries a 4.4 GPA and enjoys singing. Then meet Theresa Steiner, who has cerebral palsy. Confined to a wheelchair and unable to speak, Steiner expresses herself by maneuvering a toggle stick with her head, which types her thoughts onto a small screen and produces a computer-generated voice. Hippensteel describes Steiner as "one of the most amazing people I've ever met." Steiner conveyed her sentiments about Hippensteel

> *Paul proclaimed a **pure** grace: no mixtures, no additives, **no alterations**.*

through her communicator: "You are my sunshine." An unlikely pair? Absolutely. "When God creates a friendship, it's not about how fast you can run or even if your body works well. It's not about friendship plus any requirements. Nothing is needed but willing hearts," says Hippensteel. "That is what God uses."[1]

The apostle Paul likely would have agreed. Some things stand on their own. Grace, for instance. "God's way of making us right with himself depends on faith—counting on *Christ alone*" (Philippians 3:9 TLB; emphasis mine). Paul proclaimed a pure grace: no mixtures, no additives, no alterations.

Do we have "pure grace faith"? Before you are too quick to answer, make sure a "Jesus +" religion hasn't crept into your faith.

Jesus + evangelism: *How many people have you led to Christ this year?* Or:

Jesus + contribution: *Are you giving all you can to the church?* Or:

Jesus + mysticism: *You do offer penance and pray to the Virgin Mary, don't you?* Or:

Jesus + heritage: *Were you raised in the church?* Or:

Jesus + doctrine: *When you were baptized, was the water running or still? Deep or shallow? Hot or cold?*

Legalism. The theology of "Jesus +." Legalists don't dismiss Christ. They trust in Christ a lot. But they don't trust in Christ alone.

We're tempted to dismiss legalism as harmless. After all, legalists look good. They act religious. They promote morality and decency and good living. Is there any harm to their teaching?

Paul responds with a resounding "yes!" He reserves a biting tone for the legalists, those who were demanding that people had to be circumcised to be saved. "Watch out for those who do evil, who are like dogs, who demand to cut the body" (Philippians 3:2 NCV). Ouch! Can you hear the intolerance in those terms? "Evil." "Dogs."

Why the intensity? Why so harsh against legalists? Simple. Self-salvation makes light of our problem.

On our own, we're spiritually sunk, my friend. As sunk as Carly Boohm was . . .

Carly Boohm, as told to Gail Wood
Christianity Today
July 2003

"Now remember, you're to stay out of the river," my mom reminded me for the hundredth time as I left that morning.

"Don't worry, Mom," I said before driving off to meet my friends in the church parking lot. My youth leader and several friends from my youth group were heading to the Wenatchee River to take part in a relay race. I wasn't going to be in the race—I'd never even been in a canoe before. My job was to take the canoes and paddles from point to point along the river in the car.

When we arrived at the river, someone suggested we go canoeing. My friends weren't experienced whitewater canoeists, but they had some canoeing experience. Besides, we'd only be floating for about two miles. So I called my mom and asked for permission. After I told her we were going to put the canoes into the water right in front of a park, she reluctantly agreed.

I carefully stepped into the aluminum canoe along with Ruben and Marya—two of my best friends. Excited, we pushed off from shore and began what was supposed to be a short trip. But the rushing water was higher than usual because

of heavy rains and melting snow from the sur-
rounding mountains.

We hadn't gone far before the canoe over-
turned, dumping us into the freezing water.
Although the swift current quickly pulled us
downriver, we were able to swim to a little sandy
island, and Ruben pushed the canoe to shore.

I was shivering and scared and didn't want to
get back into the canoe. But we still needed to get
back to the other side of the river, where we'd started. And since we'd never be able to swim across
the swift waters, the canoe was our only choice.

"Come on, Carly," Ruben insisted.

Reluctantly I climbed back in, and we started
down the river. As we approached a bridge, we
suddenly turned sideways. Ruben shouted to
Marya to paddle harder, but we were sucked
toward a pillar of the bridge. We hit it hard, and
the canoe capsized, throwing Ruben and Marya
into the river.

The force of the water wrapped the over-
turned canoe around the pillar like tinfoil, and I
was pinned about three feet underwater. I
couldn't break free or raise my head above the
water. My lungs ached for air. I was trapped.

"Please, God, Save Me"

Ruben and Marya were swept downriver, and as
soon as they were able to struggle to shore, they

began screaming for help. I managed to lift my hand in a plea for help. Shocked bystanders on the bridge could barely see it above the rushing waters. Someone called 911.

It was 2:50 in the afternoon. A frantic race to save my life began.

Meanwhile, Everett Gahringer, a volunteer for the sheriff's department, was running his boat upriver. He saw people on the bridge frantically pointing at me and the submerged canoe.

I was drowning. "Please, God, save me," I prayed. "Don't let me die."

Mr. Gahringer wrapped a rope around the canoe and tugged, hoping to jar me free. But it was useless.

Another sheriff's boat arrived—one with a much more powerful motor. But the river was too strong. Mr. Gahringer went to shore, thinking it was over.

It was now 3:15, and I had been underwater for twenty-five minutes.

Everyone thought it was too late to save me— except for one medic on shore who had been praying. That medic, Shawn Ballard, knew the icy waters would slow my body functions, which would extend my chances of surviving. He knew I might be able to go a little longer without air.

"Let's try again," Mr. Ballard yelled through cupped hands.

Then a fire truck with a winch and cable rolled onto the bridge. Volunteers wrapped the cable around the canoe. Slowly the canoe rose, and my body was freed—only to be swept quickly down-river. Mr. Gahringer revved his motor and raced downstream and was able to pull me in his boat.

It had been forty-five minutes since our canoe had flipped and trapped me underwater. I still wasn't breathing, and my heart had stopped.

Inside the ambulance, Mr. Ballard used shock pads to restart my heart. Several times. It started . . . stopped. Started . . . stopped. "God, please save this girl," he prayed.

My body temperature was 72 degrees when I arrived at the hospital.

My parents drove four hours to the hospital, praying the whole way. When they walked into the intensive care room, I was still unconscious. The doctors told them I probably wouldn't live through the night and if I did, I'd be little more than a vegetable.

But four days later I slowly raised my arm and waved to my mom, who was sitting by my hospital bed.

A Long Recovery

Whenever people hear my story, they talk about what a miracle it is that I'm alive. The governor of Washington named me the "Miracle of the

Season." Larry King interviewed me on his television program, and my story has been on *Dateline NBC, The Today Show*, and the *It's a Miracle* program.

And it's true: the fact that I am alive is a miracle.

I've always shared my faith in Jesus and invited people to come to church with me, but I've had a lot more opportunities to talk to others about him since the accident. My dad says God spared my life so I can tell others about his love. So I try to do that whenever I can.

When somebody becomes a Christian, people say they got "saved." I like to think God has saved me not just once, but twice.[2]

100

Are we not like Carly was? Are we not equally helpless and hopeless? Like Carly, we are submerged—not in water but in sin. We need to be lifted up—not out of the river but out of our failures. "There is no one who always does what is right, not even one" (Romans 3:10 NCV). Like Carly, we're trapped.

Separating you and God is not three feet of water but an insurmountable flood of imperfection and sin. Do you think that by virtue of your moral muscle you can push the vessel aside and swim against the racing river to shore? Do you think your baptism and Sunday attendance will be enough to save you?

Legalists do. They miss the gravity of the problem. By offering to help, they not only make light of sin, they mock God. Who would look at the cross of Christ and say, "Great work, Jesus. Sorry you couldn't finish it, but I'll take up the slack"?

The Christian trusts a finished work. "Gone are the exertions of law-keeping, gone the disciplines of legalism, gone the anxiety that having done everything we might not have done enough. We reach the goal not by the stairs, but by the lift. . . . God pledges his promised righteousness to those who will stop trying to save themselves."[3]

Grace offers rest. Legalism never does.

Your salvation showcases God's mercy. It makes nothing of your effort but everything of his. "I—yes, I alone—am the one who blots out your sins *for my own sake* and will never think of them again" (Isaiah 43:25 NLT; emphasis mine).

> God **pledges** his promised righteousness to those who will **stop** trying to save **themselves**.

Can you add anything to this salvation? No. The work is finished.

Can you earn this salvation? No. Don't dishonor God by trying.

It's not about what we do; it's all about what he does.

◐◭▽▷ ***a thought question*** ◐◭▽▷

*Do you have a "Jesus +" faith? What steps
of faith do you need to take to trust
in Jesus alone to save you?*

*Now **live** like you mean it.
Answer the questions on pages 159–160.*

chapter 11

my body is about him

Last fall, Beverly Mitchell returned to her ranch home in Douglasville, Georgia, from a two-and-a-half-week vacation in Greece and was alarmed to find the lights on in her house and a strange car in the driveway. She called the police, who went in and found Beverly Valentine living in the house. Valentine had not only taken down the owner's pictures and replaced them with her own, but she had also brought in a washer and dryer and her dog and was wearing Mitchell's clothes. In fact, she had changed the utilities to her name, ripped out the carpet, and repainted a room she didn't like.

"In twenty-eight years, I've never seen something this strange," said chief sheriff's deputy Stan Copeland.[1]

Strange indeed. She acted as if the dwelling were hers. How could she?

Or, better asked, how could we? Don't we do the same thing with God? When it comes to our bodies, the Bible declares that we don't own them. "You are no longer your own. God paid a great price for you. So use your body to honor God" (1 Corinthians 6:19–20 CEV).

(104)

Use your body to indulge your passions? To grab attention? To express your opinions? No. Use your body to honor God. "Use your whole body as a tool to do what is right for the glory of God" (Romans 6:13 NLT). Your body is God's instrument, intended for his work and for his glory.

The Corinthian Christians had serious trouble with this. When it came to the body, they insisted, "We can do anything we want to" (1 Corinthians 6:12 CEV). Their philosophy conveniently separated flesh from spirit. Have fun with the flesh.

Honor God with the spirit. Wild Saturdays. Worshipful Sundays. You can have it all.

Paul disagreed. He reminded his readers that God interwove body with soul, elevating them to equal status. Your body is no toy. Quite the contrary. Your body is a tool. "Do you not know that your bodies are members of Christ himself?" (1 Corinthians 6:15 NIV).

What work is more important than God's? Doesn't it stand to reason, therefore, that God's tools should be maintained?

You might be thinking, *Hold on there, Max. This isn't a diet book.*

You've heard it all, haven't you? Eat balanced meals. Exercise regularly. Avoid fat. Eat protein. Get rest. We've heard it all. And we've blown it all. Each of us has. To one degree or another we have mismanaged our bodies. You're thinking, *Lucado is reaching for the guilt hammer.* I'm not. You don't need a reprimand. A reminder maybe, but a reprimand? No. Yes, your abs may be a bit soft, but so is your heart. Soft for Christ. Soft for others. Otherwise you wouldn't be reading this book. Stay that way. "Workouts in the gymnasium are useful, but a disciplined life in God is far more so, making you fit both today and forever" (1 Timothy 4:8 MSG). If forced to choose, take the soft heart over the hard body.

> ***Wild** Saturdays.*
> ***Worshipful***
> *Sundays.*

But I don't think a choice is required. Maintain God's instrument. Feed it. Rest it. When he needs a sturdy implement—a servant who is rested enough to serve, fueled enough to work, alert enough to think—let him find one in you. He uses you.

Greater still, he lives in you. "Don't you know that your body is the temple of the Holy Spirit, who lives in you?" (1 Corinthians 6:19 NLT). Paul wrote these words to counter the Corinthian sex obsession. "Run away from sexual sin!" reads the prior verse. "No other sin so clearly affects the body as this one does. For sexual immorality is a sin against your own body" (v. 18 NLT).

> You **know** the sexual anthem of our day: "I'll do what I **want**. It's **my** body." God's firm response? "No, it's not. It's **mine**."

What a salmon scripture! No message swims upstream more than this one. You know the sexual anthem of our day: "I'll do what I want. It's my body." God's firm response? "No, it's not. It's mine."

Do you recognize the name Erika Harold? She was crowned Miss America in 2003 and caused a firestorm by making abstinence part of her platform. This was not an attempt to grab publicity but a courageous stand on a value instilled in her at an early age.

Penny Lent,
Christian Examiner
May 2004

How do parents raise a child so confident and mature they become Miss America? It's really quite simple, according to Donna Harold, mother of Miss America 2003, Erika Harold.

Robert and Donna Harold knew they were fight-

ing an uphill battle to keep their children grounded in faith and truth in today's culture. "It's really the grace of God that kept my kids good," she said. "But we set high standards and kept them. I was very strict. There was no bad music in our house. No alcohol. No sex. I'd tell the kids and their friends, 'If you aren't married, then no sex.' We always had lots of kids at home—eating, sleepovers—but doing everything by our standards."

After winning Miss Illinois, then Miss America and graduating from the University of Illinois, Erika applied to ten law schools and was accepted in all." She opted for Harvard, where she chose to use her $50,000 pageant scholarship for a law degree.

The fact that Erika is articulate and smart and has a lot to share with students is evident in her frequent public presentations. In school interactions Erika says she finds lots of children who feel they are mistakes and think only of their inadequacies. "But when they believe their life is meaningful, then they realize, too, they need to put it to good use," she said. "I tell them how Jeremiah 29:11 says God knows his plans for us, to prosper and not harm us, but to give hope and a future."

Erika acknowledges that she is careful about not crossing the line in secular settings, opting to keep her convictions to herself unless asked. "But all kids need to know God is wise, with a

plan," she said. "I feel we are the light of God to others, not a verse. We must embody Scriptures."

But before Erika talks to teens about sex, she said she finds it necessary to be prayed up, well caffeinated, and well slept. "I can talk anywhere on bullying and violence, but abstinence until marriage sets a much higher standard, and some people don't like that," Erika said. "I'm often warned that students may boo my commitment, but instead they always applaud."

She finds that today's teens can't often be scared by facts, but they can be inspired, be given a goal. "When we challenge them, no matter what the past is, they can renew and reclaim their future, with choices," Erika said. "I don't want to leave them with the fear of AIDS but with hope, a vision of an exciting, incredible future. I want all kids to have optimism. The saddest thing is when they wish I had spoken to them before they made bad choices that they now regret. I tell them they have the power to reclaim an abstinent lifestyle and do something positive for their future. But I don't just focus on the consequences of sexual activity; I focus on the benefits of being married."

After her crowning, Erika again made headlines when pageant officials threatened to remove her crown and scholarship unless she stopped speaking on abstinence. That, she said, was when she realized the crown wasn't the

most important thing in her life—her salvation was. "Like Queen Esther in the Bible, I realized maybe I was meant to be used of God in this conflict," Erika said. "So I remind myself I live for God's purpose, and my real crown is in heaven—one I will never lose.

"Sometimes I feel discouraged and inadequate to give kids what they need to hear," Erika says. "So I ask God to guide me. And I remember my favorite verse, Psalm 37:4, which says to delight in the Lord, and he will give you the desires of your heart. So I don't give up. I persevere.

"We have to finish our race well, because God has a bigger plan than we can conceive. In heaven, God won't ask how many times we read the Bible, but did we put our love into action? That is teaching the value of life and affirming it."[2]

Erika's right. God does have a bigger plan. He has a bigger—and better—plan for sex than we often do. God is not antisex. Dismiss any notion that God is antiaffection and antiintercourse. After all, he developed the whole package. Sex was his idea. From his perspective, sex is nothing short of holy.

He views sexual intimacy the way I view our family Bible. Passed down from my father's side, the volume is one hundred years old and twelve inches thick. Replete with lithographs, scribblings, and a family tree, it is, in my estimation, beyond value. Hence, I use it carefully.

When I need a stepstool, I don't reach for the Bible. If the foot of my bed breaks, I don't use the family Bible as a prop. When we need old paper for wrapping, we don't rip a sheet out of this book. We reserve the heirloom for special times and keep it in a chosen place.

Regard sex the same way—as a holy gift to be opened in a special place at special times. The special place is marriage, and the time is with your spouse.

Casual sex, intimacy outside of marriage, pulls the Corinthian ploy. It pretends we can give the body and not affect the soul. We can't.

The me-centered phrase "as long as no one gets hurt" sounds noble, but the truth is, we don't know who gets hurt.

God-centered thinking rescues us from the sex we thought would make us happy. You may think your sexual activity is harmless, and years may pass before the X-rays reveal the internal damage, but don't be fooled. Casual sex is a diet of chocolate—it tastes good for a while, but the imbalance can ruin you. Sex apart from God's plan wounds the soul.

Sex according to God's plan nourishes the soul. Consider his plan. Two children of God make a covenant with each other. They disable the ejection seats. They burn the bridge back to Mama's house. They fall into each other's arms beneath the canopy of God's blessing, encircled by the tall fence of fidelity. Both know the other will be there in the morning. Both know the other will stay even as skin wrinkles and vigor fades. Each gives the other exclusive for-your-eyes-only privileges. Gone is the guilt. Gone the undisciplined lust. What remains is a celebration of permanence, a

tender moment in which the body continues what the mind and the soul have already begun. A time in which "the man and his wife were both naked and were not ashamed" (Genesis 2:25).

Such sex honors God. And such sex satisfies God's children. Several years ago *USA Today* ran an article with this lead:

Aha, call it the revenge of the church ladies. Sigmund Freud said they suffer from an "obsessional neurosis" accompanied by guilt, suppressed emotions and repressed sexuality. Former *Saturday Night Live* comedian Dana Carvey satirized them as uptight prudes who believe sex is downright dirty. But several major research studies show that church ladies (and the men who sleep with them) are among the most sexually satisfied people on the face of the earth. Researchers at the University of Chicago seem to think so. Several years ago when they released the results of the most "comprehensive and methodologically sound" sex survey ever conducted, they reported that religious women experienced significantly higher levels of sexual satisfaction than non-religious women.[3]

> *Sex **apart** from God's plan **wounds** the soul. Sex according to God's plan **nourishes** the soul.*

(I'm thinking this article would be an effective evangelism tool.)

Your body, God's tool. Maintain it.

Your body, God's temple. Respect it.

"God owns the whole works. So let people see God in and through your body" (1 Corinthians 6:20 MSG).

Manage God's house in such a way that passersby stop and notice. "Who lives in that house?" they will ask. And when they hear the answer, God will be honored.

◐◭◓◑ *a thought question* ◒◭◓◑

Whether it is the way you dress
or the way you behave sexually,
are you honoring God with your body?

*Now **live** like you mean it.*
Answer the questions on page 161.

chapter 12

my struggles are about him

Nika, a vibrant eighteen-year-old
Christian, was voted Most Likely to Succeed in high school and headed off to college to pursue her dream of replacing Diane Sawyer on *Prime Time Live.* There she wrote for the school newspaper and volunteered at the campus radio station. She joined a social club, went to church, waited tables at an Italian restaurant, spent time with her boyfriend, and juggled all this while taking eighteen hours of coursework. Life was full—and full of promise.

Six weeks after her twentieth birthday, she suddenly fell on her face in her bedroom, unable to move. Lupus, an autoimmune disorder, had caused a massive brain injury, and in the time it takes to turn a radio dial, she became a quadriplegic; she couldn't move her arms or her legs. Just the week before, she had purchased new running shoes.

How do you explain such a tragedy? Is this how God honors his chosen?

And as you're thinking of Nika's situation, how do you explain yours? The tension at home. The demands at school. The words that sting and the laughter at your expense. You may not have been struck down by lupus, but aren't you occasionally struck by God's silence? He knows what you are facing. How do we explain this?

Maybe God messed up. Cancer cells crept into your DNA when he wasn't looking. He was so occupied with the tsunami in Asia that he forgot the famine in Uganda. He tried to change the stubborn streak in your father but just couldn't get him to budge. Honestly. A bumbling Creator? An absent-minded

Maker? What evidence does Scripture provide to support such a view? What evidence does creation offer?

> Can't the Maker of heaven and earth fix bad situations and prevent natural disasters? Of course he can. Then why doesn't he?

Perhaps he is mad. Did humanity cross the line millenniums ago, and now we're getting what we deserve? Such an argument carries a dash of merit. God does leave us to the consequences of our stupid decisions. Bang your head against the wall, and expect a headache. But to label him peeved and impatient? To do so you need to cut from your Bible some tender passages such as:

> GOD is sheer mercy and grace;
>> not easily angered, he's rich in love.
> He doesn't endlessly nag and scold,
>> nor hold grudges forever.
> He doesn't treat us as our sins deserve,
>> nor pay us back in full for our wrongs.
> As high as heaven is over the earth,
>> so strong is his love to those who fear him.
>> (Psalm 103:8–11 MSG)

Don't blame suffering in the world on the anger of God. He's not mad; he didn't mess up. Follow our troubles to their source, and you won't find an angry or befuddled God. But you will find a sovereign God.

Your pain has a purpose. Your problems, struggles, heartaches, and hassles cooperate toward one end—the glory of God. "Trust me in your times of trouble, and I will rescue you, and you will give me glory" (Psalm 50:15 NLT).

Not an easy assignment to swallow. Not for you. Not for me. Not for the blind man on the side of the road. When Jesus and his followers passed him, the disciples had a question.

> Your **pain** has
> a **purpose**.

> As He [Jesus] passed by, He saw a man blind from birth. And His disciples asked Him, "Rabbi, who sinned, this man or his parents, that he would be born blind?" Jesus answered, "It was neither that this man sinned, nor his parents; but it was so that the works of God might be displayed in him." (John 9:1–3)

Born blind. A lifetime of darkness. Never saw a mother smile or a sunset fade. *Who did this?* the disciples wondered, anxious to blame someone. Such a bad plight can be traced back to a bad deed. Right?

Wrong, Jesus replied. Don't search the family tree. Don't request a copy of the man's rap sheet. Blame this blindness on a call from God. Why was the man sightless? So "the works of God might be displayed in him."

Odds are, he would have preferred another role in the human drama. Compared to others, his assignment held little glamour.

"Mary, be a mother to my son."

"Peter, you'll be my first preacher."

116

"Matthew, the first Gospel? It's all yours."

Then God turns to this man. "And you?"

"Yes, Lord?"

"You'll be blind for my glory."

"I'll be blind?"

"Yes."

"For your glory?"

"Yes."

"But I don't understand."

"You'll see."

Blindness displays the works of Christ? How can this be?

I'm looking around my office for an answer. A frame displays my favorite picture of Denalyn. A metal stand displays an antique pot. My brother gave me a stained-glass window from a country church. It is displayed by virtue of two wires and two hooks. Picture frames and metal stands, wires and hooks—different tools, same job. They display treasures.

What these do for valued possessions, the blind man did for Christ. He was the frame in which Jesus' power was seen, the stand upon which Jesus' miracle was placed. Born sightless to display heaven's strength. Do you suppose the sight of his sight showcased the work of Christ?

And you? Now it gets a bit sticky. What about your struggles? Is there any chance, any possibility, that you have been selected to struggle for God's glory? Have you "been granted for Christ's sake, not only to believe in Him, but also to suffer for His sake" (Philippians 1:29)? Is it possible that through

your struggles you point others to Christ? Watching your faith shine through a crisis might be the very thing that brings someone else to God.

God will use whatever he wants to display his glory. Heavens and stars. History and nations. People and problems. My dying dad in West Texas.

> Is it **possible** that through your **struggles** you point others to **Christ**?

The last three years of his life were scarred by Lou Gehrig's disease. The illness took him from a healthy mechanic to a bedbound paralytic. He lost his voice and his muscles, but he never lost his faith. Visitors noticed. Not so much in what he said but more in what he didn't say. Never outwardly angry or bitter, Jack Lucado suffered stately.

His faith led one man to seek a like faith. After the funeral this man sought me out and told me that because of my dad's example, he became a Jesus follower.

Did God orchestrate my father's illness for that very reason? Knowing the value he places on one soul, I wouldn't be surprised. And imagining the splendor of heaven, I know my father's not complaining.

A season of suffering is a small assignment when compared to the reward.

Rather than begrudge your problem, explore it. Ponder it. And most of all, use it. Use it to the glory of God.

Nika Maples did. Hear the rest of her story in her own words:

Nika Maples
September 2004

In the intensive care unit, I overheard physicians warning of the worst: I might have as few as forty-eight hours to live. Dear friends and family clung to my hands, caressing limp fingers and offering disbelieving good-byes. I felt their tears fall on my arms and run down my wrists. Conscious, I marked the passage of time by the regularity of my heart monitor. I could not speak. I could not open my eyes.

This is suffering, I declared. *This is suffering*, I said to God. I talked to him and him alone, day after excruciating day. I continually asked my only Friend, *Why?*

"I consider that your present sufferings are not worth comparing with the glory that will be revealed in you," he answered.

I had memorized Romans 8:18 in seventh grade Bible class, not knowing what it meant. What did I understand of glory then? What did I know of suffering? But I had tucked the verse away in my heart. God was packing my spiritual suitcase for a journey across the valley of the shadow of death. When those words resurfaced, I was quiet and ready to hear his whisper.

119

"Not worth comparing," he said as he came close.

"Not worth comparing"—the words felt like breath on the back of my neck.

"Not worth comparing," I began to say as weeks passed.

I finally was tuned in to God, and I listened. Acquaintance with suffering intensified; the characteristics of glory ever deepened in mystery. Glory is God himself. Glory revealed in us is not so much the hope of heaven or miracles wondrously unfurled in our lives but the majesty of the moment when our suffering quiets us into submission, and we realize that the Creator deigns to live inside the created.

My future, my destiny, I discovered, never was a successful career but him. My purpose is God. I live, I am, and yes I move for him.

At one time, every dream I had treasured was irreparably broken. But amid the wreckage, I was at peace for the first time. In the center, I was still.

A decade has passed since those early hospital days, and doctors are astonished by my recovery. After months of grueling speech therapy and physical therapy, I eventually regained the ability to speak well and to walk, with a prominent limp and a cane. My dreams of delivering the nightly news are all but abandoned. It is

a greater honor to deliver the good news around the world. I have shared the story of God's glory displayed in my life in Japan, Australia, Germany, Canada, and Thailand. I even taught the children of missionaries in Bangkok for almost a year.

My dearest ministry today is teaching in a public high school. I earned my degree in journalism after all, and I use it to teach English, photojournalism, and creative writing. On the first day of school, I always tell my students about the day I fell to the carpet. Mouths gape, eyes widen, and teenagers sit amazed; they cannot believe how far I have come. I pray often that my example shines with the likeness of Christ.

Mirroring God has become my career plan, my life goal. Sometimes I look at the sweet faces of my students while reminding them that life can be lost in a moment, and I am overwhelmed with blessing. A God-centered life is the highest call for living, and I would not want to be living anything less.[1]

Through my dad's illness and death, God was seen.

Through Nika's struggle and recovery, God continues to be seen.

Through your problems and mine, may he be seen as well.

◑◐◓◔ ***a thought question*** ◑◐◓◔

*If your struggles are not about
you, how can you allow God to
be seen through them?*

*Now **live** like you mean it.*
Answer the questions on pages 162–163.

chapter 13

my
success is
about him

How well do you know the following people and organizations?

Wieden and Kennedy

Goodby, Silverstein and Partners

BBDO

J. Walter Thompson

How did you do? Not too well? If not, then the ones on the list are pleased. Advertising agencies don't exist to make a name for themselves. They exist to make a name for others. While you may not be acquainted with the companies, aren't you familiar with their work?

Wieden and Kennedy changed the way we viewed athletic gear with the Nike slogan "Just do it" in 1988.

"Got milk?" Goodby, Silverstein and Partners created the slogan in 1993.

"M'm! M'm! Good! M'm! M'm! Good!" Credit BBDO with the catch-phrase Campbell's Soup has used since 1935.

And "Have it your way"? BBDO came up with that line for Burger King in 1973.

You don't hum the name of J. Walter Thompson, but have you hummed the jingle his agency wrote for Kellogg's "Snap! Crackle! Pop!" Rice Krispies?[1]

We could learn a lesson from these companies. What they do for clients, we exist to do for Christ. To live "reflecting like mirrors the brightness of the Lord" (2 Corinthians 3:18 JB).

As heaven's advertising agency, we promote God in every area of life, including success.

That's right—even your success is intended to reflect God. Listen to the reminder Moses gave the children of Israel: "Always remember that it is the LORD your God who gives you power to become rich, and he does it to fulfill the covenant he made with your ancestors" (Deuteronomy 8:18 NLT).

From where does success come? God. "It is the LORD your God who gives you power to become rich."

And why does he give it? For his reputation. "To fulfill the covenant he made with your ancestors."

God blessed Israel in order to billboard his faithfulness. When foreigners saw the fruitful farms of the Promised Land, God did not want them to think about the farmer but the farmer's Maker. Their success advertised God.

Nothing has changed. God lets you excel so you can make him known. And you can be sure of one thing: God will make you good at something. This is his principle: "True humility and fear of the LORD lead to riches, honor, and long life" (Proverbs 22:4 NLT).

> **Their success**
> **advertised** God.

You may not be the richest kid in town, but you might be given a scholarship, an award, a good job, a pay raise. You may not be the valedictorian or drafted by the NFL, but you might be given friends or money or resources or opportunities. You will, to one degree or another, succeed.

And when you do, you might be tempted to forget who helped you do so. Success sabotages the memories of the successful. Kings of the mountain forget who carried them up the trail.

The student who begged for help in medical school ten years ago is too busy to worship today. Back when the family struggled to make ends meet, they leaned on God for daily bread. Now that there is an extra car in the garage and plenty of money in the bank, they haven't spoken to him in a while. When the father suffered a stroke, family members spent hours in prayer. Today he's strong and healthy and back at work. Who needs to pray?

> **Success** *gives birth to* **amnesia**.

Success gives birth to amnesia. Doesn't have to, however. God offers spiritual ginseng to help your memory. His prescription is simply "Know the purpose of success." Why does God help you succeed? So you can make him known.

Amanda Harper knows something about success—and remembers its source.

Muscular Dystrophy Association
October 24, 2003

Affected by congenital muscular dystrophy, Amanda missed two months of her senior year at Corona del Sol High School in Tempe, Arizona, due to chronic severe back pain—"off the charts pain," says her mother, Merlie. Finally, in January, she was able to return to school for the last semester of her senior year, armed with heavy

painkillers and the "blessing" of having to take only three classes.

Unfortunately, one of the classes was Mr. Brugger's creative writing class. Not that creative writing was a problem; far from it. Amanda's writings had been filling up a box on her mom's shelf since grade school, and she had won several writing awards, including the Columbia Scholastic Press Association Gold Circle Award in 2001 for a personal essay titled "If Only My Legs Worked."

The problem was that Dan Brugger insisted she write a play and submit it to the contest sponsored by VSA Arts, an international nonprofit that challenges middle and high school students of all abilities to take an artistic look at how disability affects their lives. The winning play would be performed at the John F. Kennedy Center for the Performing Arts in Washington, and the second-place work would receive a staged reading of excerpts.

Amanda freely admits she "whined and begged" to get out of the assignment. She'd never written a play before, she protested, and she preferred to write about a character's thoughts. Mr. Brugger held firm. "I remember sitting next to his desk looking at the VSA brochure, and it said you could write with a partner. I perked up," she recounts. After the teacher agreed to let her collaborate on the piece, "I went straight home and called Bethany and said, 'You have to help me graduate.'"

Bethany Andrews is another blessing in Amanda's life. The girls met doing volunteer work at the Christian bookstore where their mothers worked. "When we found out we both loved to write, it just clicked, and we started writing together," says Amanda. "She would spend the night at my house, and the next day our moms would go, 'What story did you make up this time?' We've written about ten stories together, not including our own stories."

Bethany also sports an impressive writing portfolio, including a play that was produced by her high school. Together, she and Amanda are a powerful team.

Amanda's writing "trademark" is always to include at least one character with a disability, even if disability isn't the theme of the piece. Both girls share a deep curiosity about the different ways that "God made people" and were interested in portraying "hidden disability— something that isn't out there like a wheelchair."

"Rule number one of writing is always 'write what you know,'" Amanda says with a grin. A self-described "listener who can talk to anybody," she used to be called on by the resource teachers to help calm down kids in the remedial classes. So Amanda and Bethany wrote about Haven, a high school girl who uses a wheelchair and also provides a kind of haven for other students who need a listening ear. In addition to

Haven, the play features Dominic, a high school boy struggling with the hidden disability of depression. Haven wants to go to the prom but is convinced no one will ask her because she can't dance. The two help each other, and in the end she and Dominic go to the prom together, with him declaring, "Get ready to walk and roll!"

Amanda and Bethany's play, "Get Ready to Walk and Roll," was sent to VSA literally at the very last moment, then promptly forgotten in the rush of graduation. In July, Amanda and Bethany were stunned to get a call saying their script had been selected from more than 170 works for a staged reading at the Kennedy Center on September 29. In addition to the onstage production, their prize included $500 each and a trip to Washington.

Hearing their work performed caused the girls to "cringe a couple of times, and go 'we want to change that,'" says Amanda. But public reaction was extremely positive, and several people asked if they could produce the work at their own schools. "A lot of people said it made them review what they think about disabilities."

Even though they have graduated from high school, the girls continue to write together and separately. "There are so many paths out there," Amanda muses, adding she's sure writing will be a part of whatever she does. She's thought about teaching creative writing, but at the moment her

plans are simple: to "let God guide me to the place where He wants me to be."[2]

Three thousand years ago David declared, "Riches and honor come from you alone, for you rule over everything. Power and might are in your hand, and it is at your discretion that people are made great and given strength" (1 Chronicles 29:12 NLT).

Why are you good at what you do? For your comfort? For your wallet? For your self-esteem? No. Deem these as bonuses, not as the reason. Why are you good at what you do? For God's sake. Your success is not about what you do. It's all about him—his present and future glory.

a thought question

Isn't it time to start giving God the glory for the successes he's given you? (If you don't feel you have any successes, think about the blessings in your life, or ask God to help you see clearly the ways he views you as successful).

Now *live* like you mean it.
Answer the questions on page 164.

chapter 14

upward thinking

A tall Manhattan skyscraper housed a company owned by the CEO. Everyone in the building worked for the CEO, who officed on the top floor. Most had not seen him, but they had seen his daughter. She worked in the building for her father. She exploited her family position to her benefit.

One morning she approached Bert, the guard. "I'm hungry, Bert. Go down the street and buy me a Danish."

The demand placed Bert in a dilemma. He was on duty. Leaving his post would put the building at risk. But his boss's daughter insisted. "Come on, now; hurry up."

What option did he have? As he left, he said nothing but thought, *If the daughter is so bossy, what does that say about her father?*

She was only getting started. Munching on her muffin, she bumped into a paper-laden secretary. "Where are you going with all those papers?"

"To have them bound for an afternoon meeting."

"Forget the meeting. Come to my office and vacuum the carpet."

"But I was told . . ."

"And I am telling you something else."

The woman had no choice. After all, this was the boss's daughter speaking. Which caused the secretary to question the wisdom of the boss.

And on the daughter went. Making demands. Calling shots. Interrupting schedules. Never invoking the name of her dad. Never leveraging her comments with, "My dad said . . ."

No need to.

Wasn't she the boss's child? Didn't the child speak for the father? And so Bert abandoned his post. An assistant failed to finish a task. And more than one employee questioned the wisdom of the man upstairs. _Does he really know what he is doing?_ they wondered.

I wondered too. I had been listening to this story recounted by the rabbi sitting next to me on the plane.

He had begun his tale to teach me about the Third Commandment: "You shall not take the name of the LORD your God in vain" (Exodus 20:7). "Don't think language; think lifestyle," the Jewish teacher instructed. "The command calls us to elevate the name or reputation of God to the highest place. We exist to give honor to his name."

His point was clear. The girl dishonored the name of her father, not with vulgar language, but with insensitive living. If she kept this up, the whole building would be second-guessing the CEO.

But my traveling partner wasn't finished. He scratched his bearded chin and lifted both eyebrows as he proposed, "But what if the daughter acted differently?" and then proceeded to recast the story.

Rather than demand a muffin from Bert, she brings a muffin to him. "I thought of you this morning," she explains. "You arrive so early. Do you have time to eat?" And she hands him the gift.

En route to the elevator she bumps into a woman with an armful of documents. "My, I'm sorry. Can I help?" the daughter offers. The assistant smiles, and the two carry the stacks down the hallway.

133

And so the daughter engages the people. She asks about their families, offers to bring them coffee. New workers are welcomed, and hard workers are applauded. She, through kindness and concern, raises the happiness level of the entire company.

> **But they know his *child*, so they know his *heart*.**

She does so without even mentioning her father's name. Never does she declare, "My father says . . . " There is no need to. Is she not his child? Does she not speak on his behalf? Reflect his heart? When she speaks, they assume she speaks for him. And because they think highly of her, they think highly of her father.

They've not seen him.

They've not met him.

But they know his child, so they know his heart.

By now the flight was ending, and so was my Hebrew lesson. Thanks to the rabbi, the Third Command shouldered new meaning.[1] Paul, another rabbi, would have appreciated the point. He wrote, "We are ambassadors for Christ, as though God were making an appeal through us" (2 Corinthians 5:20). The ambassador has a singular aim—to represent his king. He promotes the king's agenda, protects the king's reputation, and presents the king's will. The ambassador elevates the name of the king.

Eighteen-year-old Grace Noppert certainly has been an ambassador for Christ. During her senior year at South Dearborn High School, she was president of National Honor Society and Fellowship of Christian

Athletes and was part of the Students Against Destructive Decisions (SADD) Student Leadership Council of Indiana. "I have learned . . . that leadership is far more than a position; it is an act of service to others," Grace says. The previous summer she lived in Honduras for six weeks, volunteering as a teacher's aid and translating assistant. She says, "Anything and everything I have ever done or accomplished is because of the help of the people around me and God."[2]

May I close this book with a prayer that we also will be ambassadors who elevate the name of the king. May God rescue us from self-centered thinking. May we have no higher goal than to see someone think more highly of our Father, our King. After all, it's not about . . . well, you can finish the sentence.

"Do you know how the story ends?" the rabbi asked as we taxied to a stop. Apparently he had a punch line.

"No, I don't. How?"

"The daughter takes the elevator to the top floor to see her father. When she arrives, he is waiting in the doorway. He's aware of her good works and has seen her kind acts. People think more highly of him because of her. And he knows it. As she approaches, he greets her with six words."

The rabbi paused and smiled.

"What are they?" I urged, never expecting to hear an Orthodox Jew quote Jesus.

"Well done, good and faithful servant."

May God sustain you until you hear the same.

◄◊♥► *a thought question* ◄◊♥►

If you are an ambassador for your Father,
what impression do other people get of God?

Now live like you mean it.
Answer the questions on page 165.

🔷🔷🔷 *Notes* 🔷🔷🔷

Chapter 1: Bumping Life Off Self-Center

1. Erin Curry, "World's Fastest Teen: Allyson Felix Takes Silver Medal," *Baptist Press News*, August 26, 2004. Reprinted by permission of Baptist Press, www.bpnews.net.

Chapter 2: Show Me Your Glory

1. Tom Knott, "Admiral Deserves a Salute from All," *Washington Times,* June 17, 2003.

2. Krista Bjorn, "Iowa Teens Put Their Faith in Action," *Merced [CA] Sun Star,* August 14, 2004.

Chapter 3: Divine Self-Promotion

1. Exodus 33:18; 1 Kings 8:10–11; Ezekiel 3:23; Luke 2:9; Hebrews 1:3; John 1:14; Mark 9:1–13; 2 Peter 1:16–18; Matthew 16:27; Revelation 21:23.

2. Aimee Courtice, "Walking with Austin," Young Life's *Relationships,* Spring 2003. Used by permission.

Chapter 4: Holy Different

1. Darren Brown, ed., *The Greatest Exploration Stories Ever Told: True Tales of Search and Discovery* (Guilford, CT: Lyons Press, 2003), 223.

2. Jerry Bridges, *The Pursuit of Holiness* (Colorado Springs: NavPress, 1978), 64.

3. Habitat for Humanity and Emma Arthur, December 2004. Used by permission.

Chapter 5: Just a Moment

1. Tamara Shaya, "Ohio/Indiana Super Teens," *Next Step Magazine*, March/April 2004. Used by permission.

2. Greg Asimakoupoulos, "A Walk to Remember," *Breakaway*, August 2003. Copyright © 2003 Focus on the Family. All rights reserved.

Chapter 6: His Unchanging Hand

1. Rick Reilly, "Sportsman of the Year: Lance Armstrong," *Sports Illustrated*, December 16, 2002, 56.

2. Keith Niebuhr, "Stronghold," *St. Petersburg Times,* August 16, 2004. www.sptimes.com/2004/08/16/oly-men-gymnast/graphic.shtml.

3. Joseph Rojas of Seventh Day Slumber. Used by Permission.

4. J. I. Packer, *Knowing God* (Downers Grove, IL: InterVarsity Press, 1973), 71.

Chapter 7: God's Great Love

1. Amy Morsch, as told to Dean Nelson, "The Least of These," *Christianity Today*, February 1999. Used by permission of Heart to Heart International.

2. Used by permission of Casas por Cristo. www.casasporcristo.org

Chapter 8: God's Mirrors

1. Dictionary of American Naval Fighting Ships, Office of the Chief of Naval Operations, Naval History Division, Washington, http://www.ibiblio.org/hyperwar/USN/ships/dafs/DD/dd400.html.

2. Genine Antonelli, "For Catholic High Teen, Volunteer Work Is 'an Extension of My Faith,'" *Lancaster [PA] New Era,* October 5, 2002. Copyright © 2002 *Lancaster New Era.* All rights reserved.

3. From *Campus Life* magazine, Christianity Today, Int'l., © 1996. Used with permission.

Chapter 9: My Message Is About Him

1. Mike Flanagan et al., *The Complete Idiot's Guide to the Old West* (New York: Alpha Books, 1999), 171–73.

2. This story was reprinted with permission of the AmazingKids! Web site: www.amazing-kids.org. AmazingKids! is an educational, nonprofit organization dedicated to inspiring excellence in children and helping them realize their own amazing potential. To read more stories about amazing kids like Austin-Nichole, browse the AmazingKids! of the Month story archives on their Web site at www.amazing-kids.org/kids.htm.

3. Rick Atchley, *God's Love Does Not Change,* audiocassette of a sermon, Richland Hills Church of Christ, Fort Worth, Texas, July 28, 1996.

Chapter 10: My Salvation Is About Him

1. Laura Hippensteel. Used by permission.

2. Carly Boohm, as told to Gail Wood, "Don't Let Me Die," *Christianity Today,* July 2003. Used by permission.

3. J. Alec Motyer et al., *The Message of Philippians* (Downers Grove, IL: InterVarsity Press, 1984), 166.

Chapter 11: My Body Is About Him

1. "Stranger Takes Over Georgia Woman's House," October

22, 2004, copyright 2004 Associated Press. All rights reserved.

2. Penny Lent, "Miss America 2003 Makes Teens, Abstinence Her Platform," *Christian Examiner,* May 2004.

3. William R. Mattox Jr., "Aha! Call It the Revenge of the Church Ladies," *USA Today*, February 11, 1999, 15A.

Chapter 12: My Struggles Are About Him

1. Nika Maples. Used by permission.

Chapter 13: My Success Is About Him

1. Ad Slogans Unlimited, http://www.adslogans.co.uk/hof/hofindx1.html.

2. Christina Medvescek, "Teen with Congenital MD Wins National Playwriting Award." Reprinted with permission of the Muscular Dystrophy Association, www.mdausa.org.

Chapter 14: Upward Thinking

1. With appreciation to Rabbi Daniel Thomson for sharing this story.

2. Grace Noppert, "Ohio/Indiana Super Teens," *Next Step Magazine*, March/April 2004. © 2004. Used by permission.

appendix

live like you mean it

Journal Questions

◊◊♡▷ **Chapter 1** ◊◊♡▷
bumping life off self-center

Why is it so easy for us to be focused on self?

_____

_____

_____

_____

_____

_____

_____

*Who is the most unselfish person
you know? What impact does
it have on others?*

_____

_____

_____

_____

_____

_____

◀◆▼▶ **Chapter 2** ◀◆▼▶
show me your glory

Consider your prayer life.
Put a percentage in front of each one.

_____ praising God for who he is (adoring him, giving him glory)

(143)

_____ thanking God for what he has done

_____ interceding for the needs/concerns of others

_____ praying for God's work and will to be done on the earth

_____ admitting/confessing your own failures and sins

_____ asking God to change you

_____ requesting that God give you material things or change your circumstances

_100%_ Total

What steps can you take to make your prayer life become more God-honoring, more others-focused, and not so self-centered?

_____

_____

_____

_____

_____

_____

Describe a specific situation in your own life this week in which you saw the glory of God displayed.

(144)

_____

_____

_____

_____

_____

_____

_____

_____

◊▲▼◊ **Chapter 3** ◊▲▼◊
divine self-promotion

*In the presence of what famous person (living or
dead) would you be starstruck and speechless?
Why are you so awed by that person?*

(145)

_____

_____

_____

_____

_____

*Do you live in awe of God?
Are you dumbstruck by his glory?
Why or why not?*

_____

_____

_____

_____

_____

_____

*Which phrase best fits how you
give glory to God or praise God?
Circle any and all that apply.*

serious and somber

enjoyable and satisfying

an act of duty

an act of passion

celebration

obligation

fun

loud

quiet

best alone

best in a crowd

tearful

moving

boring

other (specify):

◊♦♥◊ **Chapter 4** ◊♦♥◊
holy different

List all of the ways you are different from God.
How are "his ways not your ways?"

147

What's the most amazing work
you've ever seen God do?

How does the truth of God's power
encourage you in any current
difficulties you are facing?
Where do you need the Lord to
show himself strong on your behalf?

_____

_____

_____

_____

_____

_____

_____

◇◆◇◆ **Chapter 5** ◇◆◇◆
just a moment

If you could go back in time and change some decision(s) in your past, what would you do differently and why?

_____

_____

_____

_____

_____

When in your life has heaven seemed most real and this world had its loosest grip on you?

_____

_____

_____

_____

_____

_____

Think of the promise of eternity—affliction traded for glory. How, if at all, does that divine assurance help you?

_____

_____

_____

_____

_____

_____

_____

◁△▽▷ *Chapter 6* ◁△▽▷
his unchanging hand

Why do you think some people fall apart at the least pressure or change in their routine, while others face huge change all the time, almost without blinking?

_____

_____

_____

_____

(151)

List the ways your life is changing. How can the scripture, "Jesus Christ is the same yesterday and today and forever" (Hebrews 13:8 NIV) give you comfort?

_____

_____

_____

_____

_____

_____

_____

_____

What steps can you make to give God
control over all the changes in your life?

_____

_____

_____

_____

_____

_____

_____

_____

◁◆▽▷ **Chapter 7** ◁◆▽▷
God's great love

*Why do some people have a harder time
believing in God's love than others?*

_____

_____

_____

_____

_____

_____

153

*When have you felt as though your
failures might somehow exhaust
the limits of God's love?*

_____

_____

_____

_____

_____

_____

*What circumstances or life situations
cause you to doubt God's love?*

_____

_____

_____

_____

_____

_____

_____

_____

_____

*When, if ever, did God's love
become more than just a word
or an idea—when did it become
deeply personal and real to you?*

_____

_____

_____

_____

_____

◇◆◇▷ **Chapter 8** ◇◆◇▷
God's mirrors

*What role do you think God may
be giving you to play in this
great drama called life?*
(Hint: Look at your gifts, abilities,
opportunities, experiences, and passions.)

_____

_____

_____

_____

_____

*What do you mirror to others and promote-your
team? Your school? Yourself? Your God?*

_____

_____

_____

_____

_____

_____

_____

_____

Are you willing to serve God wholeheartedly, and reflect his glory, even if that means you don't get the attention and acclaim others get?

_____

_____

_____

_____

_____

_____

_____

◁◁▽▷ **Chapter 9** ◁◁▽▷
my message is about him

In your opinion, how much play-acting goes on among Christians? How much of what we do is intended largely to call attention to ourselves?

_____

_____

_____

_____

_____

_____

157

If you were to take a two-week road trip with five strangers, what might they conclude about you and your deepest convictions at the end of the journey?

_____

_____

_____

_____

_____

_____

_____

How does it make you feel to realize that God doesn't need us to do his work; rather, he allows us to work with him—not because we are so competent, but because he is so kind?

If other Christians in the world imitated your practices and habits of "sharing the good news of Jesus," how effectively would the message be spreading?

◖▲▼◗ **Chapter 10** ◖▲▼◗
my salvation is about him

*Is it difficult for you to accept the news that salvation
is a free gift—that you
cannot earn it? Why or why not?*

*How does your understanding of the
message of Christ need to change?*

*Who do you know needs to
hear about Christ's unconditional
love and acceptance?*

_____

_____

_____

_____

_____

_____

◁◆▽▷ **Chapter 11** ◁◆▽▷
my body is about him

What do you sense God is saying to you about how to view your body?

_____

_____

_____

_____

_____

_____

(161)

What steps can you take to use your body for God and his purpose?

_____

_____

_____

_____

_____

_____

_____

_____

◊◊◊◊ **Chapter 12** ◊◊◊◊
my struggles are about him

What is the biggest ordeal you've ever faced?
The greatest tragedy?

_____

_____

_____

_____

_____

_____

How can you walk through your
immediate hardships
in a way that glorifies God?

_____

_____

_____

_____

_____

_____

_____

How would you respond if an non-religious friend were to ask you, "Why does God allow his people to experience such hardship and suffering?"

_____

_____

_____

_____

_____

_____

_____

_____

(163)

How can you be an instrument of compassion and encouragement in the lives of loved ones to help them glorify God in their hardships?

_____

_____

_____

_____

_____

_____

_____

_____

_____

◁△▽▷ **Chapter 13** ◁△▽▷
my success is about him

How has God given you:

Success?

_____
_____
_____
_____
_____

Blessings?

_____
_____
_____
_____
_____
_____
_____
_____
_____